BLACKOUT

The Concordia Computer ~~Riots~~

Tamara Brown
Kym Dominique-Ferguson
Lydie Dubuisson
Mathieu Murphy-Perron

PLAYWRIGHTS CANADA PRESS
TORONTO

Blackout: The Concordia Computer ~~Riots~~ © Copyright 2023 by Tamara Brown, Kym Dominique-Ferguson, Lydie Dubuisson, and Mathieu Murphy-Perron
First edition: May 2023
Printed and bound in Canada by Imprimerie Gauvin, Gatineau

Jacket design by Dimani Mathieu Cassendo
Photo on pages 144–145 courtesy of Concordia University; photos on pages i, ii, and 146 courtesy of Canada Wide Feature Service

Playwrights Canada Press
202-269 Richmond St. W., Toronto, ON M5V 1X1
416.703.0013 | info@playwrightscanada.com | www.playwrightscanada.com

LIBRARY AND ARCHIVES CANADA CATALOGUING IN PUBLICATION
Title: Blackout : the Concordia computer riots / by Tamara Brown,
    Kym Dominique-Ferguson, Lydie Dubuisson, and Mathieu Murphy-Perron.
Names: Brown, Tamara (Author of Blackout), author. | Dominique-Ferguson, Kym,
    author. | Dubuisson, Lydie, author. | Murphy-Perron, Mathieu, author.
Description: A play.
Identifiers: Canadiana (print) 20230146430 | Canadiana (ebook) 20230146937
    | ISBN 9780369104168 (softcover) | ISBN 9780369104175 (PDF)
    | ISBN 9780369104182 (EPUB)
Classification: LCC PS8603.R6938 B53 2023 | DDC C812/.6—dc23

Playwrights Canada Press operates on land which is the ancestral home of the Anishinaabe Nations (Ojibwe / Chippewa, Odawa, Potawatomi, Algonquin, Saulteaux, Nipissing, and Mississauga), the Wendat, and the members of the Haudenosaunee Confederacy (Mohawk, Oneida, Onondaga, Cayuga, Seneca, and Tuscarora), as well as Metis and Inuit peoples. It always was and always will be Indigenous land.

We acknowledge the financial support of the Canada Council for the Arts, the Ontario Arts Council (OAC), Ontario Creates, and the Government of Canada for our publishing activities.

Canada Council
for the Arts
Conseil des arts
du Canada

ONTARIO ARTS COUNCIL
CONSEIL DES ARTS DE L'ONTARIO
an Ontario government agency
un organisme du gouvernement de l'Ontario

Canada

ONTARIO | ONTARIO
CREATES | CRÉATIF

Blackout is dedicated to Terrence Ballantyne, Allan Brown, Wendell K. Goodin, Omowale Indongo, Rodney John, Douglas Mossop, and all those who fought alongside them, past, present, and future.

Ase

Anti-Blackness, anti-Indigeneity, and other forms of racism persist in part because of the idea that there is one version of history that white people have exclusive dominion over. It is expressed through the Eurocentric dismissal of oral histories and the reliance on the written word as irrefutable truth. It is expressed through an almost scientific reliance on the "white encoders of history" to tell us "truths," even when we accept that there are obvious reasons as to why we should not rely on white supremacist historians to teach us African history.

—Sandy Hudson, "Indigenous & Black Solidarity in Practice: #BLMTOTentCity"

FOREWORD

BY RODNEY DIVERLUS

There are few things more powerful than that of student power; and at the intersection of student and blackness this power is often at its most potent. In 1960, it was four post-secondary students from the North Carolina Agricultural and Technical State University who staged the first Greensboro sit-in, some of the first protests of the Civil Rights Movement in the United States, that eventually paved the way for the formal end of the Jim Crow era. In 1976, it was secondary school students in Soweto whose direct confrontation with the terroristic police apparatus of Apartheid South Africa led to the beginning of international calls for the downfall of the regime. And in 1969, at Montréal's Sir George Williams University, present day Concordia University, six Back Caribbean students spurred a campus-wide movement to address anti-Black racism within their educational spaces. This singular act of resistance fuelled a campus-wide series of direct actions whose impacts spanned beyond the institution; actions that drew international attention to the realities of being Black in Canada. By extending the narrative beyond their individual treatment to a broader indictment of societies' attitudes and treatment of Blackness, these youth revolutionaries demystified the pervasive myth of Canada being a haven for marginalized individuals—a bastion of Black inclusion.

Canada, as a political project, was founded on violent colonialism and anti-Black racism—so too are its storied institutions. In this context, post-secondary institutions become political battlegrounds where power and the disenfranchised are often in conflict; where those in the margins are regularly confronted with the realities of being relegated to those disparate corners. *Blackout* reminds us of how fragile that relationship is, and that ultimately, what is at stake when we dare to challenge that power.

Blackout is both an act of remembrance and call to action; a manifesto of sorts filled with poetic incantations, fervent care, and ancestral reverence, with a tinge of a subtle rhythmic militancy. In this work, words carry with them the power to agitate, to ignite a deep sensorially-driven, empathetic audience experience. We feel for our characters because they are us, Black folk navigating North America in the past and in the present.

Blackout presented possibility; an imaginative and speculative exploration of what it could've have been like to be those six students grappling with the elicits of anti-Black racism. Students who, when presented with the choice of the status quo and resistance, chose the latter. Students who galvanized an entire community towards action. Their story fitting within a lineage of Black student revolutionaries across the diaspora.

Blackout gives voice to the nameless; referred simply as Students 1–6, they represent more than the original students who instigated these protests, but really represent the core of Black youth and student-led reclamation of power. They represent any and all individuals who resist the status quo. There is specificity through anonymity, a reminder that you too, the Black reader, the Black audience member could be one of them.

Blackout presents to us a series of missed priorities. Of institutions who value equipment over lives, optics over justice, silencing over change.

But *Blackout* is not about the "them," but instead, the "us." This work asks the question, quite audaciously, whose campus is this? These facilities, these books, these classrooms, these libraries and theatres, are they not ours?

And at its core, *Blackout* is a textual altar for freedom fighters past and present. An homage of sorts for the memory and legacy of those who said enough is enough. And risked their futures, for our future. We thank you. We honour you. Ase.

Rodney Diverlus is a Haitian Canadian multi-hyphenate artist and artivist whose work samples from dance, theatre, media, and public-arts-based interventions. They are co-founder of the Wildseed Centre for Art & Activism, Black Lives Matter—Canada, Black Lives Matter—Toronto, and was previously Lead Canadian Organizer for the Black Lives Matter Global Network Foundation. They choreographed the premiere production of Blackout.

PLAYWRIGHTS' NOTES

It was a cold morning in 2018 at
Black Theatre Workshop's rehearsal hall,
room #460, 3680 rue Jeanne-Mance,
but the idea stepped into the universe
on February 11, 1969.

Surrounding a table filled with poets, actors, directors, writers,
this *Blackout* braintrust was formed.
Tableau D'Hôte Theatre assembled this team
to tell this story,
but the history would be anew
because archival historical facts
continued to be flawed,
written by the colonialist powered ones:
it was skewed.

With the freedom to view those facts,
the writers came together
They then dipped into the wells of
the memory of their mutual ancestors.
Using found fact and their melanin's
collective remembrance
To bring truth from mind, to page, to stage
Honouring six students from 1969 . . .
Their cry to be heard
A desire to be seen
Respected and acknowledged
Sir George Williams Campus,
was never the same
and . . . neither were they . . .

Racism is ugly. Canada is not untouched by this odious truth. As you the reader experience this play, whether through words on these pages or mounted on multiple stages, we ask you to be of open mind and con-science. Listen to the humanity translated through history, a history that would have many believe that a simple sit-in protest on the ninth floor of the Sir George Williams Campus at 1455 de Maisonneuve Blvd. West, was a violent riot.

It was not.

—Tamara Brown, Lydie Dubuisson,
Kym Dominique-Ferguson, Mathieu Murphy-Perron

Blackout: The Concordia Computer ~~Riots~~ was first staged by Tableau D'Hôte Theatre on January 30, 2019 at the theatre formerly known as the D. B. Clarke Theatre* at Montréal's Concordia University, in the very building where the events that inspired the play transpired fifty years prior to its staging.

Shauna Thompson: Player/Student/Anchor/Voice 1
Sophie-Thérèse Stone Richards: Player/Student/Anchor/Voice 2
Kym Dominique-Ferguson: Player/Student/Anchor/Voice 3
Gita Miller: Player/Student/Anchor/Voice 4
Michelle Rambharose: Player/Student/Anchor/Voice 5/Administrator 2
Dakota Jamal Wellman: Player/Voice 7/Anderson/Black Professor 2/ Fulton/White Student/Lawyer/Administrator 3
Lucinda Davis: Player/Voice 8/Sylvie/Dean Madras/Rae/Black Professor 1/D. B. Clarke/O'Brien/Chair
Maryline Chery: Chorus 1
Marie Hall: Chorus 2
Justin Johnson: Chorus 3
Jahlani Knorren: Chorus 4

Writing unit: Tamara Brown, Lydie Dubuisson, Kym Dominique-Ferguson, and Mathieu Murphy-Perron, with contributions from Michelle Rambharose, Warona Setshwaelo, and Dakota Jamal Wellman

Director: Mathieu Murphy-Perron
Choreographer: Rodney Diverlus
Assistant Directors: Tamara Brown, Shanti Gonzales
Stage Manager: Kate Hagemeyer
Apprentice Stage Manager: Kate Stockburger
Dramaturgical Consultant: Diane Roberts
Lighting Designer: Audrey-Anne Bouchard
Sound Designers: Rob Denton, Elena Stoodley
Set Designer: Sophie El-Assaad
Costume Designer: Noémi Poulin
Projection Designer: Jaclyn Turner

Makeup Designer: Pamela Warden
Assistant Lighting Designer: Étienne Mongrain
Assistant Designer: Nalo Soyini Bruce
Production Manager: Nikita Bala
Technical Director: Martin Nishikawa

The text includes found material from the following sources, indicated through quotation marks throughout the play: *The Georgian* newspaper, City of Montréal court transcripts, interviews from Dorothy Eber's *The Computer Centre Party*, minutes and notes from Concordia's Records Management and Archives department, and various transcripts of news reports.

Blackout was developed with the collaboration and support of Playwrights' Workshop Montréal.

* D. B. Clarke was the Principal (now known as the President) of the university in 1969 during the student uprising and was responsible for calling the riot police on the protesters. As a result of the staging of *Blackout* and of the labour and recommendations of Concordia's Task Force on Anti-Black Racism, the university formally apologized in October of 2022 for their mishandling of the race-based student complaints and subsequent outcomes of the protests, and has begun the process to rename the theatre. At the time of printing, the new name has yet to be chosen, but the bust of D. B. Clarke has been removed from the lobby.

BLACKOUT CASTING AND STAGING NOTES

The Players: The narrative of *Blackout* is consciously given from a Black perspective and centres Black experiences within the action; therefore it is imperative to cast racialized actors from the African diaspora for the Players and Chorus. Whenever possible, the people who are ideally suited to participate in the ritual storytelling of the play are those who can claim a connection to and authentically represent the students of the time. These students hailed from the many islands in the British West Indies (such as Trinidad and Tobago, Jamaica, Barbados, Guyana, and others) and came to Canada to study at Sir George Williams alongside Black Canadian and Black American students. Given that most French-speaking students from islands such as Haiti and Guadeloupe would most likely have attended one of Montréal's other francophone universities, their presence among the protesters has not been represented.

The Players will introduce themselves to the audience by name in the second scene of the play.

The Chorus: Through drum, dance, and breath, the Orishas are present as witnesses on both a spiritual level and an elemental level as part of the environment of the play, impacting the flow of action and the players around them both individually and collectively as appropriate. An excellent reference for their function within the play is the Ancestors from the 2015 NAC English Theatre / Centaur Theatre Company co-production with Black Theatre Workshop of Djanet Sears's *The Adventures of a Black Girl in Search of God*. Though their movements are not codified within the text itself, they are nevertheless ubiquitous and a subconscious reminder to the students both of their innate belonging in the universe itself and in their ancestral connection to the Continent. As initiators of the ritual medicine play the Players themselves are aware of the presence of the Chorus that they have called upon, however the students within the story are un- and subconscious of their presence and impact; they are felt on a molecular and personal level according to their particular temperament and behaviour.

Accents and dialects: Where players' lines have been written phonetically, it is intended to highlight when the music of the language, their accents, idioms, and the vernacular of the islands is present. It is important that the students do not all come from the same island and that when they talk amongst themselves, they retain the proximity to their own culture above assimilation into the predominant Québec society. They might have varying levels of success at code switching in "mixed company." The phrasing, vernacular, and idioms can be adjusted to accurately reflect how each student expresses themselves. The origins and dialects of the students in the original production were determined by each actor's personal connection to a particular island.

For example, in the original production:

Player 1: a student from Jamaica
Player 2: a student from Trinidad and Tobago
Player 3: a JamHaitian student (from Jamaica and Haiti)
Player 4: a local multi-generational, bilingual Canadian Black student born in Little Burgundy
Player 5: a student from Barbados
Player 6: exists at the crossroads between the world of the students and the spiritual world. They might be a student from Guyana and/or they might also be a conduit for Eshu, within the world of the play.
Player 7: a masculine elder and griot
Player 8: a feminine elder and priestess

White costume elements and props: In the original production, the Players who played white characters such as professors, administrators, students, journalists, and more, wore white costume pieces such as gloves and used white props as signifiers.

Text: Words and phrases in **bold** represent unified speech. A forward slash (/) represents the start of an overlap with the following line of dialogue.

ACT 1

SCENE 1

PLAYERS 6, 7, and 8 begin the chant in the dark as the lights gradually rise. The players should begin to be visible by the name Eshu.

PLAYER 7, 8
Bara suayo
Omonia lawana mama kenirawo e
Bara suayo
Omonia lawana mama kenirawo e
Obbara suayo eke **eshu** oddara
Omonia lawana mama kenirawo e

CHORUS
In the beginning / Il était une fois

PLAYER 8, 7
I / and I
Loved I / Feared I
Healed I / Hurt I
Remembered I / Forgot I

PLAYER 7, 8, CHORUS
AM (Ase)

PLAYER 7, 8
Desperate for control / For certainty
But entanglement / Is inevitable
Cannot eviscerate / Self
All is Ase

PLAYER 6
(appearing at the name Eshu)
Il était une fois . . .
En 1969

PLAYER 6, 8
Les papiers d'ordinateurs flottaient tel que la neige
Qui flottait au début de la première neigé

PLAYER 6, 7, 8
It was beautiful!

CHORUS
: . . until smoke . . .

PLAYER 7
Until blood curdling screams took hold of throats

PLAYER 6
It was beautiful . . . until
Pigs perceived monsters and lit barbecues nine stories high.
PLAYER 6, 7, 8
Il était une fois

PLAYER 8
Un ouragan se levait soudainement aux Caraïbes
Shango lançait son défi crunk de guerre
PLAYER 7, 8
Ogun stoked the flames of his forge
Oshun arrêta sa collecte de miel
PLAYER 6, 8
The whipping of the wind peaking at moonrise was an omen from **Oya**
Ils s'inquiétaient pour leurs enfants
**"Our children's lives are in turmoil
We must send our protection!"**

PLAYER 6
Once upon a time
A woman was arrested at the movies for sitting in the white section
A teen was shot for playing dice in the park
An actor was cuffed on a bus for fitting the description
A dancer got her arm broken for saying
"I'll meet you at the station"

PLAYER 8
Once upon a time the children of our wombs
who held our fingers in tightly clenched fists
became seven headed demons in the eyes of the other

CHORUS 1
Mais de quels droits tissent-t-ils ces histoires
CHORUS 3
Des mensonges
CHORUS 2
des répliques malhonnêtes
CHORUS 4
Ils ne savent rien de nos dieux

PLAYER 8
Qui ont pris le temps de saisir chaque étoile
Et les insérer dans les fronts de nos bébés précieux

PLAYER 6
This is a once upon a time
in a land far away from home
Where they were treated as humans
as Men and Women
as whole People

PLAYER 7
This is a once upon a time
in a land that boasts a railroad "underground" in their pride-filled history saying
"Canada was instrumental in the freeing of people from slavery!"

CHORUS 1
Extending lying treaties
CHORUS 2
Enslaving and massacring the Panis
CHORUS 3
Rewriting its own history
CHORUS 4
Continuing in its savagery

PLAYER 6
This is a once upon a time
in a computer lab
on a ninth floor

PLAYER 7
Injustices dealt
Betrayal felt

PLAYER 8
Fluttering computer data cards fly from windows
Snow that will never melt

PLAYER 6
Fires that blaze
Batons swinging freely
Every crack eroding our health
Voices screaming: FREE ME! *(Ensemble echo whispers)*
This injustice creates a hell
where a human becomes a monster
in the eyes of a pig

who can't see the world
any further than its snout

CHORUS
Once upon a time
PLAYER 7, 8
Il était une fois
PLAYER 6
Once upon a time

SCENE 2

Ensemble moves through the space, and throughout time, as though summoned to partake in something sacred and urgent.

PLAYER 6, 7, 8
Our story starts in April of 1968

PLAYER 6
But it could also be 2018, 1989, or 1734. The place: Montréal. The events take place here in this very building, in the university formerly known as Sir George Williams, a.k.a. our very own Concordia *(Ensemble echo whispers)*, but it could just as easily be at any other esteemed institution of higher learning. The time and place have both nothing *(Players echo whisper)* and everything *(Chorus echo whispers)* to do with what you will witness today.

After finishing the final exam for Zoology 431, seven West Indian students approach the dean of science to bring forth thirteen claims of unfair treatment by their professor, out of which three were inherently racist by nature.

PLAYER 6
Their names are:

PLAYER 1
Terrence Ballantyne
PLAYER 2
Allan Brown
PLAYER 3
Oliver Chow
PLAYER 4
Kennedy Frederick
PLAYER 5
Rodney John

PLAYER 7
Douglas Mossop
PLAYER 8
Mervyn Phillips

PLAYER 6
We speak their names now in power and with respect. We will not presume to step into their shoes, but rather pay them honour and tribute. You might attribute them to us, but you could just as easily call us

PLAYER 1
Fredy
PLAYER 2
Viola
PLAYER 3
Andrew
PLAYER 4
Pierre
PLAYER 5
Majiza
PLAYER 6
Bony
PLAYER 7
Anthony
PLAYER 8
or Nicholas

PLAYER 1
Shauna
PLAYER 2
Sophie
PLAYER 3
Kym
PLAYER 4
Gita
PLAYER 5
Briauna

PLAYER 6
Michelle
PLAYER 7
Dakota
PLAYER 8
Lucinda
CHORUS 1
Maryline
CHORUS 2
Marie
CHORUS 3
Justin
CHORUS 4
Jahlani

PLAYER 6
That's up to you

PLAYER 7, 8
What's important is that

PLAYER 2, 3
They came with accents
And melanin and Afro hair

PLAYER 4, 5
They had names and dreams
And they were smart

PLAYER 1
Black brains eager to learn and grow

PLAYER 2
Black brains standing their ground on foreign soil

PLAYER 6, 7, 8
They came, they studied, they toiled

PLAYER 1, 3, 5
They handed papers with Black hands

PLAYER 4, 2
Same papers as white hands

PLAYER 1
They dared to ask

PLAYER 1, 2, 3, 4, 5
Who's really in charge here?

PLAYER 1
Well here is what happened

PLAYER 3
We spoke up but you wouldn't listen

PLAYER 4
We acted and you ran the other way

PLAYER 2
Let them burn, they chanted

PLAYER 3
We heard them all chant

PLAYER 5
Let them burn, they chanted

PLAYER 7
This is what happens when a dream goes to jail, when a city forgets its mistakes

CHORUS
We see the Fear of a Black Nation

PLAYER 1
Violently seething is white frustration
At the loss of rich dividends acquired from Black importation
No longer freely theirs since the days of the Plantation
Ended by the arrival of Black Liberation

PLAYER 2
From this moment we see the birth of fear

PLAYER 5
From this moment we see its insidious growth

PLAYER 6, CHORUS
From this moment we see its imprint on concrete, minds, students, lifetimes

PLAYER 7
From this moment we see how it drives hate

PLAYER 8
From this moment we see how it lives on

PLAYER 1, 4, 6
and on

ALL
and on.

SCENE 3

STUDENT 4 and the others are already seated in class three rows from the back. There are empty seats around them. No professor in sight. The demonstrators (teaching assistants) are seated in the front row. Just as STUDENT 4 checks their wristwatch, STUDENT 1 rushes in and takes their seat beside them.

STUDENT 4
Well this is one for the history books . . . are you okay?

STUDENT 1
It's fine.

STUDENT 3
Don' worry, the professor hasn't arrived yet. And they can't understand us when we chat patois anyway. A wha gwan?

STUDENT 1
Me alright.

STUDENT 4
I've never seen you get to class exactly on time before. What happened?

STUDENT 1
Babylon was—this police officer was giving me trouble on my way here. Me did haffi show him me visa.

STUDENT 4
But you had it with you, right? You gonna be okay?

STUDENT 1
Me just get fed up sometimes. I bust me rass for me studies, and fi wha? Him cyan' even trouble himself to come to work on time and do the job them pay him to do!

STUDENT 5

Eh heh . . . true talk, yes? I had a question to ask him about something he said in the last lecture, in case it comes up on the test.

STUDENT 1

Well don't expect any help from his wutless teaching assistants.

STUDENT 2

Lower your voice nuh . . . yuh want Pierre over dere to report your name to de demonstrators or what?

STUDENT 3

You gwen get a H on your next exam if you don' watch youself.

STUDENT 2

Is just a joke to you? Already we four minutes past the hour and we ain't even start as yet.

STUDENT 1

But last week when Mervyn got to class just one minute late, they wouldn't let him in. They don't care that him never missed class or been late before, even though he's working to support his family while still in school.

STUDENT 2

I don't know, rules is rules. Back home school was very strict, more than here. High standards are important . . . but yes, they should be applied equally to everyone.

STUDENT 3

The man can't even tell us apart . . . that is probably as close to equal treatment as we gwen get from him.

STUDENT 4

I know but that's just the way it is here sometimes, you might have to jump through extra hoops to get where you're going. But it's easier when you just keep your head down and focus on being your best. You'll see.

STUDENT 5

That is true talk, yes? Nothing worth having comes easily.

Lights out, a movie starts.

STUDENT 1

You see? Is another movie! You know say him not even coming in today! I must be some kind of jackass working this hard to be a doctor when I could be a university professor and make a whole heap of money to do not one rass ting.

STUDENT 4

Sure but getting sour over it won't change things; they can't hear your meaning when you get emotional. If we have an issue, let's just write a letter and report him to the head of his department or something.

STUDENT 1

No, you not hearing me! Them so quick to call us lazy monkeys, but every single one of us is working hard for this sloppy education. I have never gotten such low grades in my life as I do in this class, and this is my favourite subject! It don' mek no sense . . .

STUDENT 5

True! I think I put more hours into this class than any of my other ones, but my grades don't show it.

STUDENT 1

Why are we working so hard and paying more money than everyone else just to get back less? It don' seem to make a difference no matter what the BUMBOKLAAT we DO—

STUDENT 2

Would you lower your voice, na. They already don't take us seriously and laugh at how we does talk, but all ya ready to buss one big set a profanity in the place?

STUDENT 4
Careful, you know we have to work twice as hard / to get half as far as it is.

STUDENT 1
To get half as far. Yes I know, thank you mummy. Hol' on, hol' on.

SYLVIE rushes in, sits beside STUDENT 1

Hello Sylvie, how are you this morning?

SYLVIE
Salut, everyone . . . Oh thank GOD we only have a movie today. You think anyone noticed I was late?

STUDENT 5
I'm sure you'll be fine

SYLVIE
You're right. Of course I'll be fine. Professor Anderson never gets mad when it's white students who enter late. Merde, I've already seen this one— in last year's class. I should have just stayed in the library instead! I swear if I end up having to take this class a *third* time my dad's going to kill me.

STUDENT 1
Well, did you ever think that maybe the problem isn't *just* with you?

SYLVIE
How do you mean?

STUDENT 1
Do you really think that he's that good of a professor?

SYLVIE
I do get better grades in my other classes . . . Tsé, I was beating myself up all this time for being stupid, but . . . it's the material that's all over the place. It's not fair, j'viens toute mêlée . . . trust me I already know that none of this stuff will even be on the final.

STUDENT 5
No no . . . I remember it perfectly, last week he specifically told us to focus on—

SYLVIE
I'm just telling you—

STUDENT 1
Funny you should say that, because we were just talking about— I want to try something, just as a test to see whether or not he even reads our work at all.

STUDENT 4
What are you up to now?

STUDENT 1
Just a little experiment to see how things really work around here. I bet you Sylvie and I could hand in the exact same paper, and then you'd see what I'm talking about.

STUDENT 3
We should all do it, what we have to lose?

STUDENT 1
So what do you say, Sylvie? Are you in?

SYLVIE
Uh, okay . . . what's the plan?

SCENE 4

A week later. STUDENT 1, STUDENT 3, *and* SYLVIE.

STUDENT 1
How much did you get?

SYLVIE
I got a ninety. Finally!

    Beat.

Wait, how much did you get?

    Beat.

STUDENT 1
Sixty-eight.

SYLVIE
What?

STUDENT 3
The same thing happened to me too.

SYLVIE
But I don't understand. I . . . I copied from you.

STUDENT 1
You got marked as a human being. Us? Not so much.

SYLVIE
Wow.

STUDENT 3
Wow indeed.

Enter students.

STUDENT 4
So . . . you get back your grades?

STUDENT 1, 3, SYLVIE
Yes.

STUDENT 4
And?

STUDENT 3, 6
(sucks teeth)

STUDENT 5
Dreeeeeaaaad.

STUDENT 4
I did better than last time . . . at least.

STUDENT 1
Did the white student you paired up with do worse than you? Then I wouldn't brag about it.

SYLVIE
I feel awful, this is so unfair. I can't even enjoy my good grade anymore! C'est-tu fucké, quoi . . .

STUDENT 1
Oh you got that right. He thinks that our melanated skin precludes us from fair grading. But mark me, I am going to get into medical school because my family is counting on me.

STUDENT 5

You said you got better grades this time around, but I didn't.
Whappen? Maybe it's not about skin colour as much as being from
foreign?

STUDENT 4

I don't know sometimes, it depends . . . All I'm saying is this is Canada
so be careful. Racism is . . . tricky. You won't get far if you alienate
people along the way.

STUDENT 1

How are we supposed to react? Our families sent us here to get an
education, not to play around. We did not come from Port-au-Prince,
Kingston, Georgetown, or some back-a-bush place to only be sent
down a path that leads to expulsion.

STUDENT 4

Well I wouldn't go around calling Little Burgundy back-a-bush if I
were you, but I get your point . . .

SYLVIE

Whoa . . . I honestly had no idea. You never talk about this stuff.

STUDENT 5

Just . . . try to see things from our perspective, Sylvie. How much do
you actually know about what it's like to be us?

STUDENT 3

You have any idea what it's like to deal with this kind of racism day in
day out? It exhausting sah!

STUDENT 6

You may not witness it, but that doesn't mean it isn't happening.

SYLVIE

But . . . *(pointing to STUDENT 4)* like they said, this is Canada!

STUDENT 6
Canadians love holding onto a past that has long since been for-
sworn. But do they really know their history and what's been done?
To children like Olivier Le Jeune, to communities like Amber Valley?
Two hundred years of slavery lie between. They love to say they're
not as bad as some other ones . . . but look at what they just did in
Halifax, to Africville! What kind of country does that to its own
citizens? I guess some folks can't get a win for themselves without
sabotaging us first . . .

Some students: Oooohh . . .

STUDENT 2
I think we should get more evidence . . . make absolutely sure we have
all our ducks in a row first, you know?

STUDENT 4
That's the only way we're going to be able to make any kind of case.

SYLVIE
I believe you, but it's hard to believe that Mr. Anderson would deliber-
ately do something like that. I didn't think he could have a—comment
on dit . . .

STUDENT 3
A racist bone in his body?

SYLVIE
Oui, that's it.

STUDENT 5
So . . . you know that's not actually a thing, right?

SYLVIE
I didn't mean literally. I mean . . . at least he's probably not trying to be
malicious?

STUDENT 4
He probably isn't . . . and that's the worst part.

STUDENT 2
It's like he made up his mind about us before he ever read a word we wrote.

STUDENT 1
How can anyone who's biased in their thinking be able to see clearly? Take my brother right here, what do you think they see? Someone who is going to rape their women and sully their purity?

STUDENT 3
I ask myself who the hell would want to have those clear women, they ain't got no curves and just a flat batty?

SYLVIE
Hey, c'est pas drôle, ca.

STUDENT 5
True that!

SYLVIE
Just because Anderson might be racist doesn't mean you can hate all white people.

STUDENT 5
True that!

SYLVIE
I mean, it's not like he said the word ni—

STUDENT 4 *stops* SYLVIE. *Discomfort.*

STUDENT 3
Nobody said anything about alla yuh, so why you don't just let them mek them point an' take it easy.

STUDENT 1
Friends, we need to take a stand.

STUDENT 4
Okay but what kind of stand, exactly?

STUDENT 5
Something, anything! I know you're as tired as I am of the way he treats us.

STUDENT 2
And these grades . . . I mean, we have to do something!

STUDENT 4
Yeah, I know . . . it's just . . . you really don't realize what we're about to get ourselves into. They're . . .

STUDENT 1
Steel up yuh spine nah! Justice is blind.

STUDENT 6
And with a sword, she swift.

STUDENT 4
I—it's just . . . a lot more complicated than you'd think.

STUDENT 5
I can't just sit here and do nothing!

STUDENT 1
So we all agree?

STUDENTS
Yes, man!

STUDENT 6
Justice is coming with one lash like: SHABOOYAH!!!

SYLVIE
What's a shabooyah? Ohmygod you guys . . . what, is this another one of those "Black things" I wouldn't get?

The group starts "shabooyah"-ing back and forth at each other like a secret code until they start cracking up.

STUDENT 6
SHABOOYAH! SHA SHA! SHABOOYAH Shut it down!

STUDENT 2
Hold on, how about we just report him to the administration first and then we'll see what we can do to make things right.

STUDENT 6
You know how them people stay man . . .

STUDENT 3
Smile in your face before them stab you in the back!

STUDENT 1
Alright then let's go prepare our case, we've got to get this right.

They exit.

SCENE 5

Students march into the office of Sam Madras, Dean of Science.

STUDENT 1
Dean Madras, did you know that there is racism here at Sir George?

Beat.

DEAN MADRAS
Please come in, do tell me everything.

The students begin speaking over one another.

(aside to the audience) They spoke quite rapidly, and I wrote. I wrote and wrote and wrote it all down as best I could. I tried to capture the words coming from all different directions as faithfully as I possibly could. Here is my account of

The Case of Negro Students

STUDENT 1
Professor Anderson is so . . . *(STUDENT 2 clears throat loudly)* so . . . if only you knew how hard it is to convince anyone of what we go through on a daily basis, Dean . . .

STUDENT 5
Blood flow. And temperature. Properties and functions. I studied for two weeks for this final exam.

STUDENT 2
There was no way to prepare for that examination with this book. And the syllabus . . . we covered more advanced concepts for our O-levels back home!

STUDENT 1
Our voices are inaudible here, so all that is left for us to do now is to use your / voice, your words.

STUDENT 5
Mr. Anderson mentioned the topics that would be covered and though I noted them quick, I studied them slow. I memorized hard, paced myself soft. I know I've got this: blood flow and temperatures, properties and functions— Organelles. Blood flow—wait—organelles? —No, this can't be right—organelles.

STUDENT 2
He suggests books for further reading that aren't even available at the library!

STUDENT 5
Fifty-five questions on organelles. Thirty-five words or less to explain blood flow and temperature. Thirty-five words or less for all that I know but fifty-five questions more for all that I don't. Thirteen days spent preparing for this moment. Not even one moment when this topic was ever announced.

STUDENT 2
We didn't receive our December examination marks until after the second quarter, so we had no idea of where we stood going into finals. Don't you think this is unacceptable, I mean we're doing everything we can to get into medical school!

STUDENT 5
A moment, my moment of panic. My blood flow. My temperature. No properties. No functions. I'm blindsided hard, but I ain't about to be soft. Mr. Anderson is quick / but we ain't slow.

STUDENT 3
I do not say this lightly, Dean Madras: Professor Anderson is a buffoon. Truly.

STUDENT 2

How am I supposed to become a good doctor when the teacher is absent, and when he deigns to even attend class at all, it's only with a mess of half-finished ideas and . . . arbitrary grading methods?

STUDENT 3

He cannot even define buffer. A buffer, of all things! I don't like to speculate but might he be . . . at times . . . impaired / when he comes in to work?

STUDENT 6

His assistants are no better: two utterly incompetent junior demonstrators who talk non-stop but can't answer our questions. What is the point of a class where students may not ask questions? Somebody should light a fire / under 'em and—

STUDENT 1

Dr. Madras, the definition of prejudice is, "A preconceived opinion not based on any reason or actual experience." It wasn't until I arrived in Canada that my fellow students and I discovered that here we are simply "Black" to you all. What a bizarre phenomenon: we call ourselves Trinidadian, Jamaican, Haitian, Guyanese, and more. Ultimately, Professor Anderson has failed us all and we have been forced to copy each other's papers to prove it.

DEAN MADRAS

(showing notes) Does this contain the essence of your grievances?

STUDENT 1

The essence of our grievances? *(aside)* Is there anything left to say?

STUDENT 3

(aside) Just one thing: Every time his gaping mouth opens, I hope for a nebula black hole implosion to occur and for his molecular structure to swiftly vacuum itself into the dumbfounded void that is the space between his two auricle and his skull, because our entire planetary

consciousness would be better off without him. While you're at it, them two junior demonstrators, them can go chuck off of Mont Royal and land in a macca bush and die from exposure to this weather they call a "mild winter."

STUDENT 1
(back to Madras) No. This does not sum up the essence of our grievances.

STUDENT 2
But in the interest of civility and laying out the facts it will just have to do, Dean Madras.

STUDENT 4
More or less.

STUDENT 1
Right, more or less.

> *The students file out of the office.*

> *During the next line* STUDENT 6 *catches* STUDENT 4's *eye and stays behind.*

DEAN MADRAS
Your voice is absent from this. Is there anything else that I've missed or would you prefer to remain anonymous?

STUDENT 4
It's . . . just . . . why won't he even call any of us by our first names like the other students? I know it seems like just a small thing, but the detachment—no, the fake politeness is what bothers me, I guess. On the surface it seems respectful: no presumption of familiarity. But that just makes it stand out more when compared to the rest of our class-mates. Who are individuals . . . and included . . . worth investing in. Well so are we . . . so am I. I have a first name . . . and it's a precious gift handed down to me in honour of a beloved ancestor. My last name

was branded onto us by a hated slave owner, generations ago. Oh, and his tone! How can someone say your name but somehow still make it sound like

CHORUS
Nigger bitch

STUDENT 6
Like some sour taste to spit out . . . Oh but when he says "Sylvie" though . . . That name is a sigh of pleasure/

DEAN MADRAS
Yes well, thank you for that Miss—uh, forgive me . . . dear.

SCENE 6

ANDERSON

Clearly this situation is in need of cold, hard facts so allow me to speak of this using my favorite analogy: molecular biology. You see, my function as a professor at this institution—or cell, if you will—is something like that of DNA in molecular biology. Like DNA, I carry instructions used to promote the growth and development of future doctors—we'll call them proteins. Proteins are integral to life much like these future doctors will be to our lives and to society. Now the students of this institution have a job something like that of RNA, which means that they use DNA as a template to go forth and become necessary proteins in our world.

However, there is some RNA that can backfire on us. They have a little enzyme that creates its own DNA and even its own instructions. Therefore, RNA must only come from the right DNA, because when RNA creates its own instructions and rules it often leads to something undesirable like that of retroviruses, leading to complications that will only hurt them.

I'm simply doing my job like good DNA, trying to send out well-equipped RNA into the world. And if there is some bad RNA among this batch, rest assured that that virus will not be permitted to affect me nor the good RNA that remains in the slightest.

SCENE 7

Students gather outside. The atmosphere is buzzing, somewhat fluid and disorganized, people are in groups laughing or arguing, some just passing through, curious. STUDENT 1 *and* 2 *confer quietly before addressing the group. There's spontaneity and excitement in the air as more people get involved. It's a serious business, but with playful energy . . .*

STUDENT 1
Friends. Family. Fellow students, we come to you bearing ill tidings.

ALL
What's going on? / I knew it . . . / No . . . how?

STUDENT 1
We have been hoodwinked! Bamboozled! Lead astray!

ALL
Come on! / No!!/ How? / What? (etc.)

STUDENT 1
Do you remember when we first accused that devil of dismissing our dreams and aspirations?

ALL
Yeah!

STUDENT 2
Remember how we thought if we just presented the evidence, that would make everything alright?

ALL
HELL YEAH!

STUDENT 4
It wasn't easy, but we put ourselves out there! . . . So now what?!!?

STUDENT 5
True say! We not just playing around here. Our futures are at stake!

STUDENT 3
We gave them everything they asked and more, I know that's right! Am I damn right, people?

ALL
DAMN RIGHT!!!

STUDENT 1
Well they've finally come to a decision.

ALL
We have a decision! / Finally! / We shall overcome!

STUDENT 2
Oh, but I'm afraid we have nothing to celebrate my friends. Ohhhh no . . . not one thing.

STUDENT 1
Wait till you hear about the decision that they passed down to us from their hoity toity little chairs looking down on our opinions and grievances . . .

STUDENT 2
If our comrade *(looks to* STUDENT 6*)* hadn't happened to come across the information we might never have found out.

STUDENT 3
Do I even want to know?

STUDENT 1
They didn't get rid of him.

ALL

What?! / Oh hell no! / Of course! / Didn't I tell you so?

STUDENT 1

Madras says they claim that our case is full of unsubstantiated suppositions! They do not believe us, friends.

STUDENT 3

They believe Anderson and his venomous words in all their proclivity!

ALL

No! / Enough is enough is enough! No justice, no peace!

STUDENT 1

That's right! We went to them in good faith! We thought that they would see us as humans but all they see when they look at us is just "Black." To them, we ain't nothing but machines.

STUDENT 2

And not only that . . . they didn't hold Anderson accountable at all. They gave him a promotion!

ALL

What! / Big surprise . . . / Shame! / No justice, No peace!

STUDENT 1

They promoted him to assistant professor!

STUDENT 1

So people, what are we gonna do?

ALL

TELL IT!!!

STUDENT 3

We're gonna do what we ALWAYS DO!

STUDENT 5
We must stick together, no matter what!

STUDENT 1
Brothers and sisters, it's time to organize! We've got to seize the day and demand respect!

STUDENT 2
Demand dignity!

ALL
YEAH!!!

STUDENT 4
We deserve respect!

ALL
HELL YEAH!!!

STUDENT 5
And we have the right to be treated same as any white student!

ALL
YEAH!!!

STUDENT 2
Though we've come here to learn I guess we'll have to do some teaching too! Show them that we haven't forgotten our history!

STUDENT 1
We know racism, we know its gaze! So why won't they believe us? How many Black voices does it take to outweigh one incompetent white one? Why won't they listen to us?

STUDENT 6
It's time to let this city, this university, and this country know, that Black folk keep telling you: I am not "your" negro!

STUDENT 1
We are Black and we are Proud! Our Blackness is powerful and we know our worth!

STUDENT 6
No justice, no peace!

ALL
No justice, no peace! No justice, no peace!

The crowd leaves, chanting "No justice, no peace."

STUDENT 1 *and 2 are left alone.*

STUDENT 1
(long beat, exhales) What do we do now?

STUDENT 2
Like we said . . . we organize. We can do this, I know we can. *(STUDENT 1 nods.)* We'll figure it out together.

They leave.

SCENE 8

ANDERSON

Now if we are to be factual rather than emotional about these matters, consider that this promotion was already in the works before this whole uproar. The announcement is only appearing now. Observe how those with no knowledge of the facts are being misled and are subsequently misleading others from being able to perceive the truth. I mean, they don't even CARE whose LIFE could be RUINED by these VICIOUS AND— *(takes a breath and clears throat)* Sir George—I mean, this cell has fostered in me a good, hard-working strand of DNA that has worked hard for years for this promotion, a DNA that is just doing their damn job! But leave it to all that confused and corrupted RNA out there creating unnecessary complications in this cell. What am I doing? It was a mistake to even attempt to engage in the first place. This is getting out of hand, I shouldn't deal with this on my own. Please excuse me.

He exits.

SCENE 9

STUDENT 1, 2, 3 and 4 walk onto the scene and set up a game of dominoes.

STUDENT 1
Double-six! Haha, I startin'!

STUDENT 3 sucks their teeth and drops their domino back into the pile. Everyone places their domino on the pile and STUDENT 3 shuffles them once again.

STUDENT 2
What we playin'? Partners or Cutthroat?

STUDENT 4, 3
Partners! / Cutthroat!

STUDENT 2
Oh gosh, all yuh can never agree on nothing eh? What you sayin' nah? Partners or Cutthroat.

STUDENT 4
I prefer to play Partners. You know me, I like the idea of working together in teams. *(STUDENT 5 enters)*

STUDENT 3
Why you always trying to rationalize things so damn logically, I'm jus here to play dominoes, why it can't just be about playin' dominoes. Me vote Cutthroat . . . every man for himself.

STUDENT 5
Yes man, Cutthroat is what I am voting for.

STUDENT 1

The tie has been broken! Come let we play and see how I go dust unoo out with a six love, one time.

STUDENT 4 reaches for the dominoes.

You know the rules: I draw double-six, I get to pick first. You zimme?

STUDENT 1 and 4 look at each other for a moment, the situation is tense.

STUDENT 3

Unoo movin' like two silverback gorillas in di freakin' jungle man! Stop it nah, we is all family so let we play some dominoes. We have enough outside pressure, all this blasted tension not gwen do we no good.

STUDENT 6 walks in but there is reticence from everyone until they pull out a hidden bottle of alcohol. Everyone cheers and starts passing it around. STUDENT 6 takes a seat a little ways from the group, pulls out a pocket knife and a stick that they whittle throughout the scene.

STUDENT 4

Rules are rules.

STUDENT 1

Rules are meant to be broken. Rules weren't meant to control us you know, we're meant to control the rules. We not afraid of di man them.

STUDENT 5 places a hand ON STUDENT 4's shoulder. Everyone starts picking their dominoes.

STUDENT 6

What you playing?

STUDENT 3

Cutthroat. First to six, win.

STUDENT 1
We need to discuss Anderson. We cyan' let this stand.

STUDENT 2
Right? We need to have a plan. What's our strategy?

STUDENT 5
True talk, but it cyah wait for once till I get a chance to play?

STUDENT 4
Maybe don't be late for the meetup next time!

> *Game starts.* STUDENT 1 *tends to slam their dominoes firmly, decisively, almost harshly onto the table. The game gets more and more intense with each slam.*

STUDENT 1
Listen, these people don't know who they dealing with. They feel like we just loud, gesticulating island people who are nothing when compared to "their Blacks."

STUDENT 3
Them white people don't give not a rass about us nor "their Blacks," everybody gettin' flop.

STUDENT 1
Look at the situation: Our people come up here as doctors, lawyers, engineers. But what kind of opportunities them give us? Same for alla we: railway porter, domestic worker.

STUDENT 3
Some of them people driving taxis here used to design buildings back home. Play yuh card nuh.

STUDENT 4
Relax, just relax . . . I'm thinking.

STUDENT 3
You think too damn much. Play yuh card!

STUDENT 4
Don't rush me!

STUDENT 1, 3
Play the card!!!

> (*TUDENT 4 slowly places their domino. They all lean forward.*)

STUDENT 4
Lock. Show your cards bredrin!

> *They do. Kmt all around.*

Rules is rules gentle people. Read the cards and weep.

> *They start another round.*

STUDENT 1
If they think we just going to let this thing go, they got another thing coming.

STUDENT 6
Yeah we should have all the Black students up and leave, lock the doors so nobody else can get out, and then throw a Molotov cocktail in they rass.

ALL (*but* STUDENT 6)
WHAT THE HELL IS WRONG WITH YOU?! / BUT WHAT DE ASS IS THIS!? / NO, DAMMIT!

STUDENT 1
That is too much!

STUDENT 6
What?

STUDENT 5
Don't joke about that!

STUDENT 3
I tell you to stop drinking the purple drink up here innuh! Them put one bag of chemicals in there.

STUDENT 2
How could that possibly help? We go find ourselves in a jail cell doing that kinda foolishness!

STUDENT 6
You call this freedom? Death before dishonour!

STUDENT 5
That is so! Past generations did their part you know, we should be willing to die for our rights for the sake of the next generation too! Like Malcolm.

STUDENT 2
Malcolm X was gunned down by his own people after having lived an almost paranoid schizophrenic life in his final years. *(pointing at STUDENT 6)* Think about it . . . it was an assassination, not a sacrifice.

STUDENT 1
We not going to throw no blasted Molotov cocktails.

STUDENT 4
At least we can agree on that much.

STUDENT 3
I for one think that is a perfectly useless way to use alcohol, what a waste nah.

STUDENT 6
You don't use alcohol in the Molotov. We fill it up with gas and . . .

STUDENT 3
I was joking! Can we get back to the game!

STUDENT 4
Right? Let's get back to the ass-cutting I am about to give all of you, I'd hate for you to miss it.

STUDENT 3
Hahaha! Who fa ass a get cut? *(slams down domino)*

STUDENT 1
Yours! *(slams down domino harder)*

STUDENT 2
All this big talk about ass-cutting . . . but I'm a surgeon, you hear. Watch meh now. *(places domino daintily)*

STUDENT 4
You're all gonna get cut! *(slams domino so hard the makeshift table shakes all the dominoes)*

STUDENT 1
Heheyyyy! *(slams domino even harder)* Done! *(pointing)* You pass, you pass, and you pass!

STUDENT 2
Buh wait nah . . .

STUDENT 4
Hold on I can play!

STUDENT 1
So yuh think!

STUDENT 3
Rasssssssssss! Them win yes.

STUDENT 1 drops the final domino in STUDENT 3's hand.

STUDENT 1
One, one, zero, zero. Ah coming for you.

STUDENT 5
Good job!

STUDENT 5 goes to high-five STUDENT 1 who just looks at them

STUDENT 1
Listen fishy. Don't come to me with that "good job." You just flip-flop so much. Who knows where you stand on anything. With that one *(points to STUDENT 4)* I know is an optimist, only wanting to hold hands and keep the faith. *(points to STUDENT 2)* Them? Everything is calculated, meticulous, strategic. Even this one here *(points to STUDENT 6)* always know they gonna come wit' some madness. But you, you just come in like a branch in the wind! Can never tell which side of the coin is going to land facing up. You even sounding like dem Canadians now when you talk, that don' worry you?

STUDENT 5
So now you questioning me? But you don't see me here all the time or what?

STUDENT 4
Oop, there it is . . .

STUDENT 5
So if I don't just go along with whatever you want, then I'm two-faced? You need to revise your thoughts one time because no one can say I am not dedicated to the cause.

STUDENT 3
True dat.

STUDENT 5
So what if I see reasoning in different people's points of view! Is not life that.

STUDENT 3
True say!

STUDENT 5
I can change my damn mind if I so choose! Why should your way of resisting be the only right one?

STUDENT 3
TRUE TALK!

STUDENT 5
Shut up nah! Why yuh always mamaguyin' me so!

STUDENT 1
Them mocking you because that is you, family! You always come with a

ALL
TRUE TALK.

STUDENT 5
So conflicting points of view means only one side can be right and true? That sounding real simple kind of like how these white people does be talking about us.

STUDENT 4
Hello! I mean who died and made you the arbiter of Blackness?

STUDENT 1
You know what, we love you and accept you the way you are.

STUDENT 5
Thank you.

STUDENT 3
Even though you move like a fish outta water!

ALL
True talk!

They begin another round of dominioes.

STUDENT 3
You know since this whole thing started, I realize I have more white hairs now.

STUDENT 1, 2
What? / How yuh mean?

STUDENT 3
Is like they white domination just a infiltrate my body! And you know what is the white hairs them is rebellious! Like, why does the white hair on my head have to stand up so straight? It come in like all the curl just gone right out of that one strand.

STUDENT 6
Like a tiki torch carrying Nazi soldier just saluting in a sea of Blackness.

STUDENT 3
Hah. I think that is how they feel.

STUDENT 4
Who? Your hair?

STUDENT 3
The administrators. Them move like them can stand above everybody else and look down on them.

Before STUDENT 6 takes another swig of rum, STUDENT 2 grabs it from them.

STUDENT 2
No, no, no! No more for you, you've had enough!

STUDENT 5
Look nuh, alla we leaders getting assassinated left, right, and centre, so we must look to the future to help us. If we don't, we go get bobolize!

STUDENT 6
Yeah . . . *(whittles stick)* The future. The Dark Mother will rise again. When the white man get cut from belly button to gullet. *(laughs)* Like a fish.

ALL
DREAD!

STUDENT 3
Yo, stop it nah!

STUDENT 6
Why allyuh getting mad at me? Yuh don't read their Bible? An eye for an eye. . . a tooth for a tooth . . .

STUDENT 2
But that is the Old Testament, yes. And as mi padna say *(indicating* STUDENT 5*)* we need to look to the future. Because the Bible also say to turn the other cheek. *(*STUDENT 4 *nods.)*

STUDENT 6
We been turning the other cheek since fo' ages! Done wit' dat now! I know who I am, do you remember who you are? We are descended from the People! Though the ancestors were taken away and defiled, they were not just slaves brought over on ships! But the settlers, they were the thieves, rapists, and murderers, all the dregs of their cities coming over here and pretending to be the bourgeoisie over in "Nouvelle France." We should Molotov the whole of them rass! Make we a repeat of that story of the woman slave, what-she-name . . .

STUDENT 1
Who?

STUDENT 6
Angélique, yes!

STUDENT 3
Who?

STUDENT 6
Marie-Josèphe Angélique. She bu'n down the whole of old Montréal, she's my hero! Did you all see that play about her few years back? It was FIYAH.

The students all look at each other quizzically like: WTF are they even talking about?

STUDENT 3
Back to dominoes please, all this fiyah talk hurting my brains.

STUDENT 1
What we SHOULD get back to is what we ah go do about this situation . . . Anderson needs to go.

STUDENT 3
For real, I don't really feel like say we can do anything about it.

STUDENT 6
(sings mockingly) Molotooooovvvv . . .

ALL
NO!

STUDENT 2
I've been thinking . . . we go need more support from the people dem.

STUDENT 3
Which people?

STUDENT 2
The rest of the students.

STUDENT 1
Okay . . .

STUDENT 3
Even the white students?

STUDENT 2
Yes. Especially the white students.

STUDENT 6
We better be careful.

STUDENT 3
Not all support is good support.

STUDENT 1
You know one of them was boasting to me about this book, *Nègres blancs d'Amérique*! Telling me how his people have suffered just like ours because they had a hard time with the English . . .

STUDENT 6
They're just mad they couldn't hang on to their colonizer power like the English.

STUDENT 5
True . . . but as long as some of them show up and follow our lead, we go be alright . . . yuh cyah just give up on people without giving them a chance.

STUDENT 6
Oh, you sweet summer child . . . bless.

STUDENT 3
White people don't stick out them neck fi anybody else but other white people.

STUDENT 4

Hear me out . . . there are some people here who get it, they're not necessarily all against us.

STUDENT 2

Then somehow we have to motivate the entire school.

STUDENT 1

Like . . . build them up into a frenzy, almost?

STUDENT 6

Yes! Get them to burn down the Hall Building one time!

ALL

NO! / NO MAN! / STOP IT, NUH!

STUDENT 2

That joke stopped being funny the first time you said it.

STUDENT 6

Fine. *(under breath)* But is not a joke I was making.

STUDENT 2

What'd you say?

STUDENT 6

Nuttin' sah . . .

STUDENT 5

ANYWAY. But true talk, we'll need a rallying cry.

STUDENT 1

Ooh, that's a good idea.

STUDENT 5

But eh eh . . . true talk don't bother yuh for your idea, ent?

ALL
Ooooooh . . .

STUDENT 1
Yuh got real jokes today, huh.

STUDENT 3
Watch it now: SHABOOYAH! *(slams domino)*

ALL
Ohhhhhhh! SHABOOYAH! SHA SHA SHABOOYAH!

STUDENT 1
SAY IT AGAIN! *(slams domino)*

ALL
SHABOOYAH! SHA SHA SHABOOYAH!

STUDENT 4
Oh yeah?? You're all gettin' your asses cut ass today, I gotta shabooyah
for ya *(slams last domino down)* THERE! *(Game over.)*

STUDENT 2
Alright, alright. Let's not get too boisterous in the place, we should
clear up and get going before we get in trouble.

STUDENT 6
The rum finish anyway.

> STUDENT 6 *leaves.*

STUDENT 1
We've got a big day tomorrow . . . if we're going to get that racist fired
then let's go home and get some rest.

> *They exit.*

SCENE 10

RAE
The Black students, they burst into my office.

STUDENT 2
We went to Principal Rae's office to make sure he knew we weren't okay with Professor Anderson's promotion.

STUDENT 1
Not one bit.

RAE
Yelling and screaming and cursing, so much cursing. Frankly, I've never heard such a plethora of profanity. It was . . . well, I don't know if you've ever sat through such aggression before, but let me tell you . . . it's pretty rugged.

STUDENT 1
(aside) Oh please, on my first day at university some students came into our classroom looking for another lecture and the professor told them to "fuck off."

STUDENT 3
Words like "murder" and "kill" are far worse than any four-letter words.

Beat.

PLAYER 6
One, two, three, four
I declare a race war
Kiss my hand, don't take a knee
Remember you must bow to me.

One, two, three, four
Letters in a curse
How many Black folk killed by cops?
Much, much worse.

One, two, three, four
Cunt, fuck, bitch, whore.
Our bodies taken, no consent.
Not sex, just rape.
Another way to flex their hate.

    Shift. STUDENT 3 *joins in.*

What's worse than a curse?
My body in a hearse
Or immersed in
Physical, cultural, spiritual violence
All of that is worse.

RAE
You're never really prepared for something like that. They were all around me, yelling at me. Asserting that "there is a man on your staff called Anderson. He is no longer there. Find a way to inform him of that fact." After they had finished huffing and puffing, I was escorted to the Hall Building.

    Students groan.

As I was saying, once they'd finished huffing and puffing, I was escorted to the Hall Building.

STUDENT 1, 2
Escorted?

STUDENT 3, 4
Escorted?

STUDENTS
Really?

STUDENT 3
Do you have no free will, Principal Rae? Did we have a gun to your back?

STUDENTS
Please.

RAE
I was surrounded. It certainly felt like an escort to me.

STUDENT 4
We just walked with you, I mean—how is that even? —Ugh.

RAE
They took me to the 12th floor. They wanted to find Professor Macleod, ostensibly to make the same demands to him as they had to me moments before. I managed to escape their grasp into a meeting of the Association of University Teachers.

STUDENT 4
Our grasp . . . ?!

RAE
Within the safety of the office—well as safe as one can be when the boss wanders into a union meeting—they happened upon Macleod mid-conversation. He was forced into the biology office where a shouting match erupted: "You're whites, we're Blacks, you're just bleeping whites!" . . . that kinda thing.

STUDENT 1
You're whites, we're Blacks?

STUDENT 4
You're just fucking whites?

STUDENT 1
That's really what you heard . . .

STUDENT 4
How can you think that's what this is about?

STUDENT 2
Why would we even care that your skin is white, that's just—

STUDENT 1
We care about what you do with your whiteness.

RAE
As it turns out, the union had recently drafted a procedure for dealing with complaints against faculty members. Not with Anderson in mind per se, but perhaps now would be the ideal moment to try it.

Faculty members run from RAE *and* STUDENTS *with a piece of paper that has the proposals/rebuttals for the conditions of the hearing.*

STUDENT 2
They suggest another hearing, a public one. This could be better than just termination, it'll give us a greater platform to expose what's been going on.

STUDENT 1
We agree.

Faculty members run back to RAE.

RAE
Yes, well . . . very well then. We have a consensus. But—

Back to STUDENTS.

STUDENT 3
But what, *exactly*?

Back to RAE.

RAE
BUT! We need formal charges in writing. Both Perry and the university have the right to an official record detailing the precise nature of these accusations.

Back to STUDENTS. STUDENTS *groan. Back to* RAE.

This much is non-negotiable.

Back to STUDENTS.

STUDENTS
Fine.

STUDENT 1
We'll place ink to paper if that makes it more real for you.

RAE
Perfect. No later than January 4th, understood? Now, here is the composition of the committee . . .

Back to STUDENTS.

STUDENT 2
No, this isn't going to work for us. There are only white professors on the committee. And that particular professor is far too close to Anderson. *(scribbles a few names furiously)* Here's our counter-proposal.

Back to RAE.

RAE
Agreed.

STUDENTS confer together.

STUDENT 1
Yes! Agreed.

STUDENT 1 reaches to shake RAE's hand, who eventually concedes.

SCENE 11

Two BLACK PROFESSORS enter. They look around surreptitiously, making sure they're alone, and then dap (elaborately, but with great warmth) before sighing heavily. They stare at one another, about to speak, then stopping. Finally:

BLACK PROFESSOR 1
Petri dish. Yes, that's what it is.

BLACK PROFESSOR 2
What's that?

BLACK PROFESSOR 1
I feel as though we're in a petri dish. Just a couple of biological anomalies waiting to be analyzed: The Black University Professors.

BLACK PROFESSOR 2
Mmhmm.

BLACK PROFESSOR 1
Hmm.

BLACK PROFESSOR 2
Shouldn't we be the microscope?

BLACK PROFESSOR 1
How's that?

BLACK PROFESSOR 2
Perry has been accused of racism. There are both academic and non-academic grounds to these charges and it is our responsibility to thoroughly analyze all factors and put forth a recommendation. We should be the microscope!

BLACK PROFESSOR 1
No, the scientists.

BLACK PROFESSOR 2
The physicians!

They both laugh in sync then sigh as the laugh comes to an end.

Or maybe we're just the petri dish.

BLACK PROFESSOR 1
Hmmph.

BLACK PROFESSOR 2
Tokens to placate the students.

BLACK PROFESSOR 1
Goddammit.

BLACK PROFESSOR 2
I know.

BLACK PROFESSOR 1
I'm no one's mascot!

BLACK PROFESSOR 2
I said I know that, but like it or not we're under the microscope now
too . . .

BLACK PROFESSOR 1
Perceptions.

BLACK PROFESSOR 2
Magic tricks and sleight of hand . . .

BLACK PROFESSOR 1
Optics.

BLACK PROFESSOR 2
A means to an end.

Silence.

But there is a way we can help . . . there must be. We may only be assistant professors for now, but we still know better than any of our peers all the ways that racial bias overwrites while it operates quietly in the back of the mind. We know these students and their struggle . . . we've been there.

BLACK PROFESSOR 1
We're still there.

BLACK PROFESSOR 2
And we can help them. Maybe Anderson is at fault, maybe he isn't. But we can still help them to navigate these halls. Teach them how to keep the vultures at bay. When to bite their tongue and when to bite necks. Not by—no. But there is a way to help.

Beat.

BLACK PROFESSOR 1
All eyes will be on us. We're about to tread a treacherous path.

BLACK PROFESSOR 2
That they will . . . that we are. But consider the alternative if we don't.

SCENE 12

All of the STUDENTS *follow* PRINCIPAL RAE, *who locks himself in the office where the meeting of the board of governors is being held. The* STUDENTS *wait outside for news.*

RAE
Dear Mr. Fulton, it is with regret that I submit to you my resignation as Principal and Vice-Chancellor. I no longer feel competent to carry out my responsibilities, but I have confidence that there are others who can do so. And with the holiday season approaching there is a brief period during which the necessary adjustments could take place.

Sincerely yours,
Robert C. Rae

FULTON
Dear Dr. Rae, I acknowledge—with deep regret—receipt of your letter of resignation. It was dealt with in camera at a meeting of the board of governors later that afternoon and resulted in the following resolution:

PLAYER 6, CHORUS
That Dr. Rae's resignation be accepted with "an expression of appreciation for the outstanding service Dr. Rae has rendered to the university."

FULTON
I wish to add my personal distress. Your resignation came not only as a great shock, but also as the loss of a very sincere friend totally devoted to the well-being and advancement of Sir George.

Yours sincerely,
F. F. Fulton
Chairman, Board of Governors

CHORUS, PLAYER 6
MINUTES OF A MEETING HELD ON THURSDAY, JANUARY 9, 1969, AT
12:00 NOON.

The chancellor reported that following the resignation of Principal Rae, Professor Clarke has agreed to accept the appointment of Acting Principal and Vice-Chancellor. The new acting principal remarked:

D. B. CLARKE
Regarding the latest developments concerning the charge of racism which has been brought against a member of the science faculty: The faculty member is not conducting classes at this time while methods of continuing these classes are under review. The students concerned have all agreed to put their charges in writing.

SCENE 13

Principal D. B. CLARKE *emerges from the meeting, only to meet a crowd of students.*

ENSEMBLE
(slowly) We. The. Undersigned. Students. Accuse. Assistant. Professor. Perry. Anderson. Of. Racism.

Beat.

D. B. CLARKE
And?

ENSEMBLE
(a little faster) We. The. Undersigned. Students. Accuse. Assistant. Professor. Perry. Anderson. Of. Racism.

D. B. CLARKE
How?

ENSEMBLE
(faster) We the undersigned students accuse Assistant Professor Perry Anderson of racism.

D. B. CLARKE
You know, specific charges are required.

ENSEMBLE
(very fast) We the undersigned students accuse Assistant Professor Perry Anderson of racism.

Beat.

D. B. CLARKE
You leave me no choice. The hearing represents Anderson's sole opportunity to defend himself. He must have this platform, as his name has been blackened all over the university and beyond. The only way forward is by a hearing regarding this charge where / you may all present the facts and evidence verbally. And to allow Anderson to present his defence. That is the only way—the only way.

    D. B. CLARKE leaves.

ENSEMBLE
(very fast, repeat until "his defence") We the undersigned students accuse Assistant Professor Perry Anderson of racism.

SCENE 14

PLAYER 6 and the CHORUS blow through the space, carrying news and rumours to the STUDENTS, who in turn pass it on to others. Finally: STUDENTS 1, 3, and 5 confront the administrator, O'BRIEN.

STUDENT 1
When we heard the echoes of

STUDENT 3
"Well now, they're threatening violence."

STUDENT 1
I took that rumour to everyone and it struck like a silent earthquake. Apparently, it was spread by another professor to his students while covering one of Anderson's classes, saying that

STUDENT 5
"Anderson will be back in a few weeks rest assured, but those Black students are threatening violence now, have you heard?"

STUDENT 1
He read it from a letter written by Dr. O'Brien. DB tells us he'll call him. He does, but O'Brien is skeptical:

STUDENT 5
"Tell them I'll get back to them."

STUDENT 1
We don't wait, we walk straight into his office asking

STUDENT 3
O'Brien, how you think we so dim?

STUDENT 5
He says

O'BRIEN
Letter? What letter?

STUDENT 1
(holds up a paper) He says

O'BRIEN
Oh, that letter!

STUDENT 1
"A risk of violence" was the exact wording.

STUDENT 3, O'BRIEN
But it's not what you think, it's about the white reaction to any demonstrations should Anderson be censured or fired.

O'BRIEN
So I really didn't mean it like that

STUDENT 1
We say

STUDENT 3, 5
"Well why dontcha prove it

STUDENT 1
Enough justification, you need to retract this misstatement."

STUDENT 5
He say

O'BRIEN, STUDENT 3
It's time for me/he to go

STUDENT 5
I place my hand on his coat

STUDENT 3
We standin' at the door

STUDENT 1
Why he feel so uncomfortable when Black folks ask for more?

O'BRIEN
The Negro students came to my office asking about a letter I'd written to Professor Anderson and whether or not it specifically mentioned the threat of violence. I did not remember writing anything like that but when we found the letter in the files, the phrase WAS there. So I apologized for the misstatement.

STUDENT 1
We want it in writing

O'BRIEN
But why?

STUDENT 3
You know why.

    Beat.

STUDENT 1
And you do not make this statement under duress.

STUDENT 5
He sits down to write

O'BRIEN
(writing) I do not make this statement under duress.

ENSEMBLE
I do not make this statement under duress.

STUDENT 1
Next day I'm served.

STUDENT 3
I'm served.

STUDENT 5
I'm served.

STUDENT 1
Our demands were met and curbed. Charges are

STUDENT 3
Extortion of a document

STUDENT 5
Unlawful confinement

STUDENT 1
Which means kidnapping under criminal code. This is how white folks deal when we point out their lies. They criminalize three Black folk

STUDENT 3, 5
For asking them to fucking apologize.

STUDENT 1
They simply lay a charge on us that only states

STUDENT 3, 5
"Well now they're threatening violence".

SCENE 15

STUDENTS gather on the mezzanine.

STUDENT 6
NAMES AND CLAIMS, PEOPLE! NAMES AND CLAIMS!
Shabooya!
Sha Sha
Shabooya!

Two beats.

STUDENT 3
Anderson failed us
He tink we stupid
He is a racist
That's undisputed!

ENSEMBLE
ROLL CALL
Shabooya!
Sha Sha
Shabooya!
ROLL CALL

BLACK PROFESSORS enter and watch.

STUDENT 4
Let's all calm down now
And don't be hasty
Decide together
Compromise, maybe?

ENSEMBLE
ROLL CALL
Shabooya!
Sha Sha
Shabooya!
ROLL CALL

STUDENT 1
Oh I don't think so
I've seen too much
Tell ME to calm down?
You out to lunch? (STUDENTS *notice the* PROFESSORS)
ROLL CALL
Shame on you!

ENSEMBLE
Shame Shame
Shame on you!
ROLL CALL (STUDENTS *close in on the* PROFESSORS)

STUDENT 5
Supposed to teach us
Came here to learn
Without protection
We're left to burn!

ENSEMBLE
ROLL CALL
Shame on you!
Shame Shame
Shame on you!
ROLL CALL

STUDENTS 1, 2
They don't respect us

STUDENTS 3, 4
Won't hear us out

STUDENTS 5, 6
Want us kept quiet?

ENSEMBLE
We'll scream and shout!

ROLL CALL
Shame on you!
Shame Shame
Shame on you!
ROLL CALL

BLACK PROFESSOR 1
We're not against you

BLACK PROFESSOR 2
We're here to help

BLACK PROFESSOR 1
We've been through this too

BLACK PROFESSOR 2
Though you can't tell

ENSEMBLE
Bullshit!
Shame on you!
Shame Shame
Shame on you!
BULLSHIT

BLACK PROFESSOR 1
Be diplomatic

BLACK PROFESSOR 2
Find better words

BLACK PROFESSOR 1
Try euphemisms

BLACK PROFESSOR 2
Don't cause a stir

ENSEMBLE
SELLOUT
You're cooning!
Shame Shame
Shame on you!
SELLOUT

BLACK PROFESSOR 1
You're young and stupid

BLACK PROFESSOR 2
With mouths like bombs

BLACK PROFESSOR 1
You'll blow yourselves / up

BLACK PROFESSOR 2
We ain't no Uncle Toms!!

ENSEMBLE
SELLOUTS
You're sellouts!
Shame Shame
Shame on you!
SELLOUTS

BLACK PROFESSOR 1
You all know nothing!

BLACK PROFESSOR 2
We came to help

BLACK PROFESSOR 1
But you're too fucking /

A scuffle breaks out. Shift.

BLACK PROFESSOR 2
Rude! Too arrogant! Too know it all, too quick to go your own way
rather than listen to a damn thing we say

BLACK PROFESSOR 1
This is to tender our resignation, effective immediately

BLACK PROFESSOR 2
to the committee set up to hear the case of the Black students against
Perry Anderson.

BLACK PROFESSOR 1
This committee was formed during a crisis situation with no clear
guidelines to follow,

BLACK PROFESSOR 2
so it seemed inevitable that unless both sides could agree comfortably
with the proposed procedure—

PLAYER 6
A'ight, a'ight, a'ight. That's enough.

PLAYER 7
For real. There's more to this story.

PLAYER 8
They weren't just "the Black university professors." Say their names.

PLAYER 7
Chester Davis

PLAYER 8
Clarence Bayne

PLAYER 8
It's easy to overlook how they were caught up in the middle of an impossible situation.

PLAYER 7
The administration had every intention to use and exploit their Blackness to get the protestors back in line.

PLAYER 8
Believing that their decree would sound more convincing coming from Black mouths.

PLAYER 7
Remember—the establishment never bestows the distinction of Black Excellence with no strings attached. It's only ever a matter of time before they come calling to collect.

PLAYER 8
Which of course they weren't going to submit to without a fight.

PLAYER 7
But the students couldn't trust them, or anyone. They had been dicked around too many times before. And the students had a right to be mad! Professors Davis and Bayne were siding with the administration by defending Anderson's right to legal representation on the committee.

PLAYER 8
Still, sometimes people can surprise you. Despite the massive blowout with the students and all the names being thrown around

PLAYER 7
Uncle Tom

PLAYER 8
Black honkey

PLAYER 7
White nigger

PLAYER 8
They eventually became two of the students' fiercest champions when the shit hit the fan.

PLAYER 7
They would travel to Ottawa to meet with government officials . . .

PLAYER 8
Urging them to not adopt punitive measures against Black international students . . .

PLAYER 7
They were on campus daily during the occupation. Passing messages along. Advocating.

PLAYER 8
When D. B. Clarke called in the riot police, they urged the cops to let them talk to the students first.

PLAYER 7
They thought they could get the students to take down the barricades and come out.

PLAYER 8, BLACK PROFESSOR 2
The administration told us, "We're sorry. We can't use your services anymore."

PLAYER 7
Later, Bayne said on national television that

PLAYER 8, BLACK PROFESSOR 2
"I believe now by the reaction of Canada and by the papers that Canada is even more racist than the United States."

PLAYER 7
He recounted how he heard one woman say that she couldn't care if they all burned.

PLAYER 8, BLACK PROFESSOR 2
Do you think she can be redeemed? She didn't care whether or not ninety-seven students burned.

PLAYER 7
With everything to lose, they still refused to be quiet.

PLAYER 8
No one ever knows what they'll really do when push comes to shove, but the professors knew this much:

PLAYER 7, 8
That the value of humanity must take priority above and beyond that of property.

SCENE 16

The day of the much-anticipated hearing committee. H110 is filled to the brink with hundreds of students. The tension is palpable. It has been ongoing for hours. There is heat, chaos, unrest. The anti-racist students are gaining ground, and they know it. Where other students are miserable, they are ecstatic. The committee chair's calls to order go unheeded. STUDENT 6 sits back and observes their strength and conviction.

STUDENT 2
Everybody! Everybody! Listen. Both sides agreed that the composition of the committee had to be agreeable both to us as well as Anderson, right? But these members here today were imposed on us. We had no say in the matter, so as far as anyone who is on the side of justice is concerned, today's hearing and this committee are totally invalid.

WHITE STUDENT
(maybe off stage/voices)
Where is your evidence? You think you can just throw the word racism around so easily? Why can't you just get over it, you're the ones that are creating division! Doesn't that make you the racists? What's your endgame here?

STUDENT 4
I understand your reticence, but . . . how can you all witness the administration acting so unjustly, and still ignore it, just . . . go on to class as usual? My friends were wrongly charged with kidnapping . . . that is not normal!

WHITE STUDENT
Cry me a river. If you're not happy here go back to yo islands, man. Stop holding the rest of us hostage with your thuggery.

STUDENT 1

You say that now but wait till the shoe is on the other foot. If they can do this to us now, what makes you think it won't happen to you later on down the road?

WHITE STUDENT

You are a small faction of thugs tarnishing the name of our university. / We refuse to have our academic year ruined because you're all too stupid to pass a zoology class.

STUDENT 5

But you're forgetting one of our basic demands: that the administration get together / both with us and with—

WHITE STUDENT

We have rights too! You're breaking the law—

STUDENT 4

Hey now! We've gone through every possible option available to us / Believe me, we've tried to do this right at every turn.

STUDENT 1

Some people would call them bunglers, others would call it incompetence. But it was neither . . . it was consciously done! / They only treated us that way because of the colour of our skin.

STUDENT 5

Real talk.

STUDENT 2

No university in the world should treat its students like this. When you have a complaint against a professor, they say they'll get in touch with you and tell you their decision. That goes without saying, right? You shouldn't have to ask for that. But the administration . . . they heard our / complaints, met together, and then presumably made a decision, but never communicated any of that to us.

WHITE STUDENT

Bullshit! If you can't keep up, you should just drop out! / Why should you get special treatment when the rest of us have to pull ourselves up by our—

STUDENT 4

Beyond the matter of whether Anderson is guilty or not, you need to address the fact that the admin has behaved unethically. But you don't bring their motives into question. You never do. Why?

STUDENT 1

You are so focused on Anderson right now. But it is your duty—no, your moral obligation to hold the administration accountable for its dealings with all its students.

STUDENT 2

The university is making world news right now for the simple reason that Black students are fighting for justice but you have the majority of white students not supporting them. Why aren't you?

Silence.

STUDENT 3

Now you don't have anything to say . . . what happened to "Oh, I want to hear both sides, I want to hear all the facts."

STUDENT 1

You're content to let injustice slide as long as you think it doesn't affect you. But all you're doing is showing the world that you are just as racist as the United States, or England, or anywhere else.

STUDENT 4

It's like you don't realize that the chips are down. Maybe you just didn't know any better, but now you do.

STUDENT 5

You have no excuse anymore, so now what are you gonna do about it?

More chants from duelling crowds. The CHAIR *calls for silence.*

CHAIR
I said that under these conditions, I would answer no questions. I just have one more thing to say however, my present condition is that I think I can sit here for about four hours, but I have a relatively weak bladder and I cannot answer for the consequences after that.

CHAIR leaves.

STUDENT 1
Will all Black people come down to the front? All those that are interested in justice, come on down.

STUDENT 6 comes forward with some papers.

STUDENT 2
Listen up, everyone . . . we recently learned two things: first, that the admin has decided to continue the committee in a closed meeting off campus.

STUDENTS boo.

The second is that—

STUDENT 6
They don't take us seriously and they never will unless we MAKE them.

STUDENTS cheer.

STUDENT 2
The second is that the administration had a security meeting but luckily *The Georgian* newspaper got their hands on the minutes.

STUDENT 3 grabs the minutes from STUDENT 2.

STUDENT 3
Listen to this, "If police reinforcements are called, they should come in through the garage and service elevator. Our most important objective must be to protect our installations. Perhaps a plainclothes constable should be in the Computer Centre as it's a very valuable piece of equipment."

Room erupts in laughter. Voice of discontentment from white student and company.

STUDENT 1
So if DB and company are interested in their precious equipment, well then they'll come to terms with us!

Cheers.

STUDENT 2
Those people who support our demands, namely one, that the administration publicly declares this committee illegal, two, that the administration meets with us and Anderson to set up a new committee, and three, that the administration drops criminal charges against three Black students, then it's time to stand up. If you agree with those demands we ask you to join us right now.

STUDENT 1
Are you prepared to stand up for your rights?

All cheer.

Are you prepared to stand up for your rights?

STUDENT 4
Yes! We're not going to let the administration push us around anymore, are we?

Cheers.

STUDENT 5
Are we going to bring this fight to the end? Right to the bitter end?

Cheers.

STUDENT 1
We're on the ninth floor in the Computer Centre; that's where we're continuing this meeting. The occupation starts now!

Arrangement mix of chants / which side are you on.

STUDENT 6
BLACK LIVES, THEY MATTER HERE!
ALL
Black lives, they matter here!

STUDENT 1
Black GRADES, they matter here!
ALL
Black grades, they matter here!

STUDENT 6
If we don't get justice, shut it down!

STUDENT 1
If we don't get justice
ALL
SHUT IT DOWN

STUDENT 5
If we don't . . . get . . . just . . . ice
ALL
SHUT . . . IT . . . DOWN

STUDENT 3
If we don't get justice

ALL
SHUT . . . IT . . . DOWN

STUDENT 6
SHUT IT DOWN?
ALL
SHUT IT DOWN!

They exit, chanting.

END OF ACT 1

EXHIBIT A3

January 10, 1969

We the undersigned students accuse Assistant Professor Anderson
of Racism.

Kennedy J Frederick

Allan Brown

Douglas Mossop

Wendel Gaudie

(Terence Ballantyne)   Sun Life
                       866 - 6411

(Roderick John)

Terence Ballantyne   1440 St. Catherine St. W., St. 314

ACT 2

SCENE 17

STUDENTS gather in the Computer Centre for inspiration, to dance and party and let off steam, they get increasingly riled up, chanting "Black is beautiful!" and "Say it loud!" and "The revolution has come!". Before they "explode" STUDENT 5 turns it into art/protest/hip hop and steps up to the mic like an MC. It's celebration, a release, an oasis in the storm. The CHORUS echoes/ amplifies.

STUDENT 5
BLACK

Black is those handsome Brothers
Swinging down the hall.
Black is the soft-spoken sisters,
Always on the ball.
Black is the courage to stand up and fight,
To answer when destiny calls.
Black is to be proud and show it
Never begging when Blackness can do it.
Black is also the bomb and the gun,
When it's time to do or be done.
Black is whatever you make it
Though for some it is newly begun.
Black is the color of a new dawn,
That will make the white sun stand back
And stare in despair and wonder,
All the beauty of light that is Black.

ALL
Of all the beauty of light that is Black.

STUDENT 6
You got the right to feel—

ALL
BLACK BOY JOY!

STUDENT 6
The revolution is—

ALL
BLACK GIRL MAGIC!

STUDENT 6
So if we want justice—

ALL
IT'S JUST US!

STUDENT 5
Brothers and sisters, I tell you now that we've got the right to be mad, and don't let nobody tell you any different! Make some noise, Black girls and boys! I said make some noise! Now somebody, anybody, everybody: SCREAM!

    Everyone screams. of joy. release. rage. taking space.

STUDENT 6
SHOUT! A little bit louder now . . . Shout! A little bit louder now . . .
The roof! The roof! The roof is on fiyah!!!! *(beat)* What!!!??? *(beat)*
It's getting hot in herre . . . Unh-huh! So come on, get your joy! *(beat)*
Look out! *(a shift)*
You'd best realize
The revolution
Can not
Will not

Be televised *(police sirens, people scatter and freeze)*
Watch. Like. Share. Fave. Retweet.
But can you see what you are looking at?

SCENE 18

JOURNALISTS gather in the Computer Centre.

ANCHOR 1
"The Black students feel power in their hands and know how to use it and they aren't / about to let it go."

ANCHOR 5
"The Black students speak with authority and conviction, at times with passion. Their style of action is bold and decisive—and utterly indifferent to the conventions of acceptable conduct within the university. One of their greatest assets is that the administration finds them completely unpredictable. Any conversation about the crisis—which is practically every conversation at the university this week—includes the warning 'but we don't know what they'll do next.'"

ANCHOR 2
"Four medical students of McGill University initiated a petition signed by four thousand fellow students stating 'We, the undersigned, wish to express our desire that the students' society of McGill University condemn the actions of the Sir George Williams University students who encouraged and participated in the destruction of university property.'"

ANCHOR 1
"The Black students feel power in their hands and know how to use it and they aren't about / to let it go."

ANCHOR 5
"Will the students provoke violence? Will they charge more teachers with racism? / If so, whom?"

ANCHOR 3
"But the students themselves are far from blameless; it is astonishing that the student council, official representatives of all the students, did not take a more positive part / in the discussions.

ANCHOR 4
"This type of action by students is likely to inflame the university and delay the possibility / of a just and equitable settlement."

ANCHOR 5
"A large number of staff and students at Sir George Williams University, probably the majority, feel that the Anderson case has been blown out of proportion to its inherent importance. They wish the Black students and the administration and the inquiry and the lawyers would just go away or at least lower their volume, / and let them get on with their teaching and their studies."

ANCHOR 2
"Many students, both Black and white, openly admitted that the specific issue was of no importance to them—they merely wanted to 'destroy the university.'"

ANCHOR 3
"Little attention has been paid to the rights of the accused—who has been nationally pilloried and humiliated without being able to defend himself, since the evidence against him has never been presented."

ANCHOR 1
"The Black students feel power in their hands and know how to use it and they aren't about to let it go."

SCENE 19

PLAYER 8

I'm an actor—obviously I'm an actor—but can I tell you how fucking
hard this play has been to work on? Researching all the disrespectful
ways in which the students were treated just a few stories above where
you're all sitting right now, reading every injustice written in black
and white, then turning on a computer to see white actors playing
cotton-picking slaves here in Montréal. And people actually defended
it! Telling us we're anti-Québec for objecting, that we should protest in
French not English . . .

PLAYER 7

We're also activists, in case you were wondering. And it's been fifty
years since people who looked like us screamed at the top of their
lungs for justice. It really took that much to ask for so little. It still does.
Just a tiny bit of justice, that they'd at least admit their mistakes . . .

PLAYER 6

"Admit their mistakes?" How about just a committee acceptable to
both sides for starters?

PLAYER 8

How does anyone even begin to have a conversation under those
conditions? If they can't even be open to hearing us without getting
defensive or insisting on having the last word, what then?

PLAYER 7

Coming together is the most important part of any political movement. We're all human beings who need each other for
comfort, for—

PLAYER 8

Comfort, right. Talk without restorative justice is worthless. I want
reparations. I WANT CHANGE.

PLAYER 6

You know what really gets to me the most? When shit hit the fan, there were people outside chanting "LET THE NIGGERS BURN!"

PLAYER 7

But there were also folks that stood up to them. In solidarity. White folk, trade unionists, and activists for an independent Québec all came together in support of this protest by yelling up to the ninth floor, "WE GOT YOUR BACK!" That gives me hope.

PLAYER 8

Did you know that when they were arrested they got most of their bail money from sex workers? People from all walks of life got involved because they understood that what was happening was not right.

PLAYER 7

Back in the day Québec sovereigntists and the Black Panther party in the States forged bonds of solidarity because they found common ground in their struggles.

PLAYER 6

We also forget too quickly the blood, sweat, and tears shed by Black women who are the silent and invisible lifeblood of the resistance, both then and now.

PLAYER 8

With every dollar donated for food, clothing, bail, and more they let the protestors know, "You are not alone," "We got your back," "You're doing the right thing," "You can relax now."

The next two lines are interwoven at the "/" Enter PLAYER 5 surrounded by the ENSEMBLE coming out from everywhere with blank white protest boards. They slowly close in around PLAYER 5, who joins in the mantra, growing frantic by the end of the repetitive piece, and breaking down.

PLAYER 4 enters, offers 5 comfort. 5 accepts, gradually giving over their body weight to 4.

PLAYER 7, 8, 4, 5
A simple act of solidarity. You are not alone. We got your back. You're doing the right thing. You can relax now. / You are not alone. We got your back. You're doing the right thing. You can relax now. You are not alone. We got your back. You're doing the right thing. You can relax now! You are not alone! We got your back! You're doing the right thing! You can relax now! YOU ARE NOT ALONE! WE GOT YOUR BACK! YOU'RE DOING THE RIGHT THING! YOU CAN RELAX NOW!

ALL
Let the niggers burn! Burn! *(repeat x8)* Let the niggers burn! Burn! *(repeat x8, underscore till out)*

PLAYER 5 collapses. The ENSEMBLE watches . . . as their wails and sobbing continue, they disperse. The CHORUS comes out to disperse the energy, 5 regains their composure.

SCENE 20

The occupation has been going on for almost two weeks. The
PLAYERS *walk in with the same box of dominoes, the apple box,*
and the makeshift table they were playing dominoes on earlier.
There seems to be a pep in their step. All but STUDENT 6 *are*
present. They set up for the game and are eating pizza at the
same time.

STUDENT 3
B'way it feels like forever since we last play a good game of dominoes,
ah missed this.

STUDENT 5
True talk, yes?

All except STUDENT 3 *look at* STUDENT 5.

STUDENT 3
Why you all still have them up fi dis! Dread! Live and let live nuh! Chuh!

They prepare to start the game.

STUDENT 2
Well, negotiations seem to be moving towards an agreement. Principal
Clarke says it shouldn't be long now.

STUDENT 1
Yes but—

STUDENT 3
What we playing?

ALL
Partners!

STUDENT 2
Yuh want to draw firs'?

STUDENT 3
Yes me friend! Thank you, I will.

STUDENT 4
Everybody agrees? Finally!

STUDENT 5
Who ha' de highest?

STUDENT 3
Double-six. Heheyyyyy!

STUDENT 4
Damn! I was hoping it'd be me this time.

> *They mix up the dominoes on the table.*

STUDENT 3
You know what, start.

STUDENT 4
Oh, really? Thanks!

STUDENT 3
Yah man, I feeling generous . . .

> *Game starts.*

STUDENT 5
I have next nah.

STUDENT 1
Yeah, maybe yuh right and this will all be over soon. I mean them accuse me and dem *(indicating STUDENT 3 and 5)* of all kinna horse

dead and cow fat, but at the end a di day the truth is what must prevail, right?

STUDENT 2 *nods.*

STUDENT 3
Weh yuh have?

STUDENT 4
Play the card man.

STUDENT 2
You'll see . . . we in the negotiating committee go meet and get everyt'ing settled.

STUDENT 1
You good wit this?

STUDENT 2
Yah man!

STUDENT 6 *hurries in but doesn't say anything to anyone, nor do they salute the group. They seem unsettled and disturbed by the calmness. They surreptitiously check the security of the perimeter. Every now and again they hear the sound of police batons striking riot shields, but no one else does. Everyone tries to ignore* STUDENT 6's *agitation*

STUDENT 1
Can we go over the terms of the agreement one more time.

STUDENT 4
This good with you? *(plays card, baton strike)*

STUDENT 3
Yeah.

STUDENT 2
Well we agreeing to come out of the Computer Centre for one.

*STUDENT 2 plays their card a little more firmly. Baton strikes.
STUDENT 6 flinches.*

STUDENT 5
Okay, but what else?

STUDENT 2
They said to make sure that we don't get violent with Professor Perry
Anderson.

*STUDENT 3 plays their card firmly. Baton strikes. STUDENT 6
flinches again. STUDENT 1, 3, and 5 stcheups loudly at this.*

STUDENT 3
Why they always coming with some violence angle. Backside man.

STUDENT 5
So what go happen next.

STUDENT 2
They go do everything possible to ensure that new committees are
formed so that the issue be given a fair hearing, and have agreed to
declare that the original committee was illegal.

STUDENT 1
Rass man . . . you think they really gonna do it?

STUDENT 2
I do. Collective action works.

STUDENT 4
Maybe. *(seeing STUDENT 6)* I still think we should be prepared for anything. Just in case.

STUDENT 5
F'real . . .

STUDENT 1
What about the charges against us . . . the kidnapping foolishness . . .
what we doing about that?

Baton strikes. STUDENT 6 *lurks in the dark, and comes out.*

STUDENT 2
Well they said our demands will be met and the charges will be dropped.

STUDENT 6
Don't believe none of that, people. Prepare to retaliate.

Baton strikes.

STUDENT 1
Retaliate . . . ?

STUDENT 2
Not this again.

STUDENT 4
No, I actually agree . . . we should have been more careful. What if this
is a trap?

STUDENT 6
How do you know you can trust everyone who's been in and out here?
(baton strikes) If you stay ready you ain't have to get ready.

STUDENT 2
Listen! Our strategy has been spot-on, they can't renege now that an
agreement is in the works.

STUDENT 3
You not lyin' still.

STUDENT 6
When did you last look outside? Do you even know what's going on anymore? Babylon coming but allyuh is too damn naive, here playing dominoes like say we back home and everyt'ing good. Everyt'ing NOT GOOD! Ah can feel it, the ancestors dem don't like this. OPEN YUH EARS! Yuh can't smell the smoke on the wind?

STUDENT 2
How you mean?

STUDENT 6
What the ass you think I mean. It's a trap. This whole damn "as good as settled" story they selling is a trap.

STUDENT 3
Nah, man. We good.

STUDENT 6
Ah telling you, they coming!

Silence.

Wake up. Ain't nobody gonna protect us but us. Grab anything you can and lay down these barricades now!

Some students build barricades.

Did yuh forget about the ancestors? Yuh siddung there just hoping for the fuckin' best! Yuh just sticking out your chins so, begging them fi cuff you one more time! Yuh must love the taste of blood in your mouth, bwoy . . . at what point in history yuh ever see them kinna people deh actually do right by we without a fuckin' fight on they hands?

Barricades are almost done. STUDENT 3 *goes back to the domino table, others follow. The baton sounds grow stronger.*

STUDENT 3
Nobody not getting in here again . . . so just easy . . . calm down.

STUDENT 2
Yes . . . please.

STUDENT 5
We still have each other. That means something . . . doesn't it?

STUDENT 6
Not if you fall asleep when you should be keeping watch! I not gonna calm down until we get up and fight for what we need.

STUDENT 4
They've messed with us so much already at this point. I was afraid of this.

STUDENT 6
Yes, man! Why believe these people here for us and that they'll be just and righteous?

STUDENT 4
I'm really scared, guys. This is bad . . .

STUDENT 6
(hearing the batons again) PLEASE. I can't do this alone, help me. Help yourselves. Before it's too late. Don't let them do you like this.

STUDENT 1
The barricades strong man! Them not getting in here.

STUDENT 3
Babylon nah come in. That gwen let them know say we mean business.

STUDENT 2
Oh god now I have a bad feeling about this.

STUDENT 5
For real . . .

STUDENT 1
Enough. We been here for nearly two weeks and . . . bu'n this, I am
going home to shower and ah coming back tomorrow morning. Is
me and dem *(points to* STUDENT 3 *and* 5*)* who have criminal charges
against we innuh! Not you! I just can't take the extra stress right now. I
not feeling good.

STUDENT 3
Cool family. *(beat)* See you in the morrows.

STUDENT 5
Ah go stay here. I meant what I said before . . . I ain't running again.

STUDENT 6
The time for running long gone, child. I can tell you this much: nothing will ever be the same, so we'd better stand fast.

STUDENT 1
I don't know what's worse—you, or dem. When you talk it make
me skin crawl, even when yuh talking sense. I gone y'hear. In the
morrows!

> STUDENT 1 *tries to leave but can't. Suddenly they can all hear,*
> *smell, and see everything* STUDENT 6 *can. On the screen we see*
> *the cops, the fire, the smoke, the chanting of the crowds outside,*
> *everything. Then the police are in full riot gear, they try the*
> *handle for the door. The door doesn't budge, they brace against*
> *it and push, the barricade shudders.*

STUDENT 1
Oh no.

STUDENT 4
Oh . . . no . . .

STUDENT 2, 3
Oh / No

The barricade shakes and rattles some more, STUDENT 1 *and 3
rush over to try and keep it steady.* STUDENT 2 *and 4 start looking for a viable escape route.* STUDENT 5 *and 6 lock eyes.*

STUDENT 5
(breathless) Oh no

ALL EXCEPT STUDENT 6
OH NO.

STUDENT 6
Oh no? Allyuh want to just stay there. Yuh think say them care bout
dem computers? Them care about them computers only marginally
more than them care about us. Dey can replace the computers them
likety split. Watch.

*STUDENT 6 gets up and goes to the computers, opens a drawer
full of data cards and takes up a stack. They go over to a
window and open it, pulling back their hand to throw the cards
out.* STUDENT 5 *stops* STUDENT 6 *and takes the stack of cards
from them with trembling hands.*

STUDENT 2
Hold on man! What you doing? *(exhales shakily)* Jeezan 'ages! Don't
provoke them and give them a reason to attack!

STUDENT 6
You ain't listening to me. They been on the attack since the beginning,
you just didn't want to believe it.

STUDENT 5 and 4 share a look, STUDENT 6 *starts to weep and
laugh.* STUDENT 5 *throws the cards out. Projection: cards fluttering in the air.*

STUDENT 3
NO, THEM GONNA KILL US!

STUDENT 2
We'll lose everything we've worked for!!!

STUDENT 3
Is whappen to you!!

> *Everyone scrambles to keep the barricades from falling except*
> *for STUDENT 6.*

STUDENT 5
I making a damn statement! After all we been through? If they go kill us, it go cost them.

SCENE 21

The STUDENTS finally chop down a door to escape the smoke. Riot police move in to forcibly put an end to the occupation, chaos ensues. The CHORUS intervenes throughout.

PLAYER 5
The building is tall
Monumental
A monstrous mountain of cold crushed stone
Cold white clouds
Obscuring its crown

PLAYER 4
Seething within its core
Its heat warms white skin
Scorches Black skin
Into a melting running river
Pooling sweeping gathering momentum
Bubbling like lava

PLAYER 2
Erupting into destruction
Paper falling like volcanic ash over the downtown streets
Like dead skin cells
The forensic evidence shedding from this concrete beastie
Collected on paper and dislodged
Drifting down like snow

PLAYER 1
Such silent destruction
Buffering silencing the dull roar
Of the crowds below
Their mouths are open tongues waggling
But not with the childish delight

Of catching snowflakes
Their words are hot and hateful, saying:
"Let the N—"
Then the carpet of silence
Shock and Horror falls

PLAYER 5
And when we turn around
Smoke billows in darkly from every crevice
Its source nowhere that we can reach
To extinguish it with what
The saliva leached out of our mouths
Into air that's thick with fear and panic
Maybe the urine soaking our pants
Or the sweat from our temples

PLAYER 3
Though we lament the bitter winters here
We still rush to break down the door
Fleeing the heat of the fire
Only to rush headlong into the burning cold embrace
Of their fear and hatred and brutality
Brandished with billy clubs
Hidden by the throng of the riot squad

PLAYER 4
Or in secret cubbies of elevators

PLAYER 5
Or in the dark of an underground garage

ALL
Where no one can hear you scream

PLAYER 3
We are paraded past administrators
Blood dripping from our contusions onto the snow

Becoming a grotesque red-carpet event
While press flashbulbs pop
And crowds cheer

PLAYER 1
A moment to honour this fallen, perishable paper
Worth more than people
Worth more than flesh
Easy to sweep away
To blot up the bloodshed
Like it never happened

> STUDENT 5 *finally sits down holding her head, winded. She closes her eyes, seeming to fall asleep.*

SCENE 22

PLAYER 6

Can we take a second to talk about this fire? The fact that even
now, fifty years later, history would have it that it was the students
who started it? That's some serious retconning shit going on right
there.

PLAYER 7

I MEAN. Smelling D. B. Clarke's betrayal and knowing full well that the
riot squad would soon be at their doorstep, the students took every
object they could get their hands on to barricade the stairwells and
entryways into the computer lab.

PLAYER 8

Just a jigsaw of desks, tables, chairs, and who knows what else.
They made the decision that nobody was going to be busting up
the Computer Centre party, except . . . no way in also meant no
way out.

PLAYER 6

Piece by piece, the police worked to dismantle the impromptu barricade. It took a few hours, but eventually every piece of furniture was
replaced by a faceless brute in a uniform ordered to round up the protestors in cuffs. Who still had no way out.

PLAYER 8

And they'd have you believe that students lit a motherfucking fire? For
what? What purpose would that have served other than to fulfill some
sort of bizarre collective suicide pact?

> PLAYER 8 *mouths "Coralee Hutchison," which gets taken up
> as whispered echoes through the space, interspersed with
> "Angélique" and "Say her name."*

PLAYER 6

As the smoke poured into halls and out of the windows, as the gathered crowds below chanted for the cops to let them burn, our students literally had to get an axe and chop down a door locked from the outside to escape the flames. Nintey-seven of 'em pouring through a single two-and-a-half foot door into the loving embrace of the police. They were smoked out, plain and simple.

PLAYER 7

Though it was tantamount to attempted murder, somehow the students were the ones who were charged and tried with arson. In the aftermath of the violence were many casualties. Marriages. Families torn apart.

PLAYER 7

A young Black woman died from a concussion weeks after being struck on the head by a billy club

PLAYER 6

while others would have theatres named after them.

PLAYER 8

Or streets.

PLAYER 6

Or metro stations.

PLAYER 8

Or statues erected in their honour. But I digress.

> STUDENT 5 *is still there, seeming asleep, but when* STUDENT
> 1 *goes over to gently shake her awake, she doesn't respond.*
> STUDENT 1 *starts to tremble violently, but doesn't allow themselves permission to weep. The other* STUDENTS *arrive.* STUDENT
> 2 *wants to go comfort 1, but is frozen in grief. They lock eyes
> with* STUDENT 4, *who runs up to 1 and enfolds them in their
> arms. After a moment, 1 can finally weep. This time 4 knows
> how to hold someone up. The chorus takes* STUDENT 5 *away,
> and once 1's tears subside, the* STUDENTS *all part ways, but 1
> and 4 exit together.*

SCENE 23

Crowd gathers outside Hall Building to comment on events.

D. B. CLARKE

About two weeks ago a number of students and other individuals occupied the university's Computer Centre.

VOICE 1

"I'm going to sue all of them. My tuition fees paid for the technology they destroyed. They robbed me of my academic year."

PLAYER 6

President of Commerce Student Association

D. B. CLARKE

The university had resisted all pressure to invoke the aid of the law and to call in the police.

VOICE 3

« J'ose espérer que nous n'allons pas nous plier devant les doléances des nonos paranos de notre société qui voient du racisme partout. »

PLAYER 6

Guy Nantel, humoriste

D. B. CLARKE

However, when violence broke out in the early hours of Tuesday, February 11, 1969, and when the occupiers began to destroy university property, the university decided that it would be derelict in its duty to the students, faculty, and the community if it took no action.

VOICE 2

"Libérez nos camarades! Their lives are worth more than your computers!"

PLAYER 6
Labour activist

D. B. CLARKE
Rather than tolerate further lawlessness, the university decided that they had no choice but to call for the assistance of the Montréal police

VOICE 1
"I'm still waiting for the official statement from the university before I pass judgment."
PLAYER 6
Becky

D. B. CLARKE
The Montréal police, with the advice of the university to avoid any unnecessary use of force, attempted to remove the barricade. At that moment a fire was set from the inside.

VOICE 4
I'm certainly not rolling in money, but you know what? I'm going to hightail myself down to the bank and have a big talk with the manager and tell him I need $2000 to pay their bail.
PLAYER 6
Irene Kon, Human Rights Activist

D. B. CLARKE
And had it not been for the courage of many policemen many of the occupiers and many innocent people would have died in the resulting blaze.

VOICE 3
"Y nous détestent nous, les blancs. Je l'ai vu dans leurs yeux. Ça faisait peur."
PLAYER 6
Policier, Matricule 211

D. B. CLARKE

About eighty individuals have been arrested and will be charged by the
university before the criminal courts. The Computer Centre has been
wilfully destroyed.

VOICE 2

We don't support this. We don't support this at all. We want people
to know that as Black Canadians, we do not condone these actions.
Violence is never the answer.

PLAYER 6

Vice-President of the Colored Women's Club.

D. B. CLARKE

Many precious records have been wantonly scattered to the wind and
hundreds of pieces of furniture have been destroyed to the tune of two
million in damages.

VOICE 4

"It's clear to us that the administration is playing a reactionary and
racist role in their attempt to railroad the Black students' quest for
justice."

PLAYER 6

Representative of the Black Community of Montréal

D. B. CLARKE

This is not a time for vindictiveness or revenge but rather for soul
searching and re-examining our values.

VOICE 1

We MUST go out of their way to be politically INcorrect at all times.
If that offends you, so be it. If you have the right to be offended, I too
have the right to offend YOU. Period.

PLAYER 6

Peter Ray

D. B. CLARKE

The university intends to act with firmness and responsibility.
Douglass Burns Clarke, Acting Principal

Applause.

SCENE 24

Next day. The stage is cleared except for one person.

ANDERSON
(reading) "Since the circumstances leading to your employment status have now changed, your suspension from teaching classes is hereby cancelled."

As I predicted, this retrovirus has only hurt itself in its attempt to gain control over this cell. Although I hope to one day forget it all, it is clear that this place will never be the same. Nor will I. I will attempt to move on and resume my position so that I can continue doing my job, but I fear this will follow me for the rest of my life. Those are simply the facts. I do not wish to speak on this any further.

SCENE 25

In court. STUDENT *1, 2, 3, and 4 are on the stand.*

LAWYER
So, you were arrested on February 11, 1969, at Sir George Williams University on the ninth floor.

STUDENT 1
Yes.

LAWYER
Are you a student at Sir George Williams University?

STUDENT 2
Yes.

LAWYER
What year?

STUDENT 3
Third year.

LAWYER
First year . . . and you are generally familiar with the events which led to an occupation of the Computer Centre?

STUDENT 4
Yes.

LAWYER
Now as I understand it, students had to sign in and out at the door. Why is that?

STUDENT 2
To wean out potential infiltrators. There are some . . . conservative students at the university who are known to get violent so we didn't want any trouble with them.

LAWYER
Did you ever observe any of these students attempt to enter by force?

STUDENT 3
No.

LAWYER
Who led the occupation? Who chaired the meetings?

STUDENT 3
It was spontaneous.

STUDENT 1
Whoever had the biggest mouth on any given day, I guess.

LAWYER
Did you ever participate in discussions about decisions that might have been made?

STUDENT 4
We all did.

LAWYER
What about?

STUDENT 2
Room allocation . . .
STUDENT 3
Where we would talk . . .
STUDENT 4
Where we would sleep.

LAWYER
Now as I understand it in the early morning of Tuesday, February 11 you made your way to the Computer Centre at 2 or 3 AM. Can you tell us why?

STUDENT 1
Negotiations had broken with the administration.

LAWYER
How did you know this?

STUDENT 3
I heard it.

LAWYER
You were not part of the group negotiating with the university?

STUDENT 4
Not directly.

LAWYER
At around 4 AM you made your way to your locker, is that correct?

STUDENT 2
Yes—

LAWYER
Why?

STUDENT 2
. . . to get my coat, gloves, and some books.

LAWYER
Why did you need your coat, your gloves, and books at 4 AM?

STUDENT 2
So they wouldn't get lost.

LAWYER
Why might they get lost?

STUDENT 1
Because . . . we were expecting trouble.

LAWYER
Who is "we"?

STUDENT 3
Everybody.

LAWYER
Who exactly is everybody?

STUDENT 1
The students . . . in the Computer Centre.

LAWYER
What kind of trouble was expected, precisely?

STUDENT 4
I don't know.

LAWYER
You had no idea what kind of trouble.

STUDENT 2
No. People who wanted to make trouble would make it. We were not . . .

LAWYER
Which people specifically?

Beat. Chorus begins to quietly chant/hum.

STUDENT 1
The administrators.

LAWYER
What exactly do you mean by trouble?

STUDENT 2

What if the administration was more interested in provoking the situation just to call in the riot squad and regain control.

LAWYER

Now you weren't the only one to head to the Computer Centre, is that correct?

STUDENT 1

Yes, it was the first time all the students moved into the computer room, the room that housed all the computers.

STUDENT 2

We didn't allow everyone to go in there during the occupation.

LAWYER

Was anything at any time planned as to what would be done if the police moved in?

STUDENT 3

Nothing was stated as such . . .

LAWYER

Was there ever any decision or any policy or plan or whatever you want to call it in existence about what would happen if the police should come in?

    Beat.

STUDENT 2

At the beginning the plan was we would . . . you see, usually we would never enter the rooms at all, we were not allowed in. But if the police moved in, we were . . . we were to go into the computer room and we thought the police wouldn't come in after us because they wouldn't— the administration wouldn't want the computers damaged . . . by the police coming in. The plan was that we would stick close to the computers . . . we believed that the computers would not be touched, so . . .

it would be the safest place for us because the machines would protect us . . . the machines . . . and if the police came in and they started . . . slamming us around, it would be clear that it was them who bashed the computers, not us. We felt . . . safer with the computers.

ENSEMBLE *quietly repeats "we felt safe with the computers" until end of scene.*

STUDENT 4
We felt we'd be more safe with the computers. As long as they remained unharmed by us, we would be unharmed by the police.

LAWYER *turns into* JUDGE.

JUDGE
Guilty. Guilty of conspiracy to commit mischief by destroying and damaging computers. Guilty of conspiracy to commit mischief by occupying the Computer Centre of the university. Guilty of conspiracy to commit mischief by causing danger to life through fire. Guilty of conspiracy to commit arson by setting fire to the Computer Centre.

SCENE 26

Three administrators, D. B. CLARKE *and two others, in the office, very late after hours. There's a thunderstorm raging outside, but the atmosphere inside is tired, wired, and maybe a bit tipsy. They're smoking and drinking at a table, surrounded by the detritus of a long meeting.*

ADMINISTRATOR 2
When shall we three meet again?

ADMINISTRATOR 3
In thunder, lightning, or in rain?

D. B. CLARKE
Well hopefully not in fire.

Administrators 2 and 3 hiss. D. B. CLARKE *sighs heavily.*

"When the hurly-burly's done, when the battle's lost and won"— Guys this is stupid. It's late, I'm tired, and no one is keeping minutes, so for once can we just get to the point?

ADMINISTRATOR 2
Fine . . . the battle has been lost by them and won by us, so what's next?

D. B. CLARKE
What are you getting at?

ADMINISTRATOR 2
What. Is. Next. How do we move forward? Institutionally? Our image as a progressive and modern university has taken a beating. In the face of this much public scandal, we can't move forward without acknowledging what's happened . . . can we?

D. B. CLARKE
Why not? I mean, look around! A Mari usque ad Mare . . . from sea
to shining "C"! Look at all of the donations we've gotten, look at these
letters of support . . .

> D. B. CLARKE *opens up a drawer and hundreds of letters come*
> *cascading out, like data cards from a window.*

"The events of the past few days are indeed regrettable and I sympa-
thized with your situation at this time," . . . or even this one, "I give full
support of the administration's intention to 'lay every possible criminal
charge' against all of them." Nobody wants to dwell on the ugly things
of the past!

ADMINISTRATOR 3
We may have doused the spirits of those terrorists, but if you look
carefully, there are still sparks smoldering out there. It wouldn't take
much to ignite them.

ADMINISTRATOR 2
So, how do you kill a flame?

ADMINISTRATOR 3
Put a lid on it. Cover it up. Smother it.

D. B. CLARKE
I thought we already agreed about the flowery language thing.

ADMINISTRATOR 3
What I'm saying is that nobody's perfect. Racism isn't as bad here as it
is in other places. We've got to leave the past behind us and start looking to all the great things still to come.

ADMINISTRATOR 2
Yes! Sir George Williams must die to live. That is how we will protect
the school.

D. B. CLARKE
We can't draft that in a press release.

ADMINISTRATOR 2
Thusly we shall move forward.

D. B. CLARKE
What exactly are you saying, dammit.

ADMINISTRATOR 3
Of course. Rebranding. Genius.

ADMINISTRATOR 2
Where is the place? Upon the heath. There to meet Loyola!

D. B. CLARKE
(to ADMINISTRATOR 3) . . . Are you going to translate?

ADMINISTRATOR 3
(to ADMINISTRATOR 2) Loyola College? I heard that it would be ceasing operations soon. How can a failing school save us?

ADMINISTRATOR 2
We need Loyola and Loyola needs us. A mutually benefiting relationship. Like a marriage.

ADMINISTRATOR 3
A merger.

ADMINISTRATOR 2
Exactly. Loyola has no charter, little funding, and cannot grant degrees. Without us, they'll be finished.

D. B. CLARKE
Now you're finally starting to make sense. So with us, they're able to carry on. We literally come to their rescue.

ADMINISTRATOR 3
Our inclusivity becomes our strength.

D. B. CLARKE
But will it be enough for a fresh start?

ADMINISTRATOR 2
By merging as one, we take on a new identity. We transform.

ADMINISTRATOR 3
We forge a new future, without history, without scandal.

ADMINISTRATOR 2
Exactly. That was then, but this is now.

D. B. CLARKE
Rebrand history.

ADMINISTRATOR 2
With lies and numbers, facts and fake news. Whatever we need to do to stifle this discord, we do it.

ADMINISTRATOR 3
One mind, one body, one heart.

D. B. CLARKE
If we can make everyone forget the discord of the past, we'll have pulled off one of the greatest cons of all time.

ADMINISTRATOR 2
Oh my god, that's it! Concord—no, Con-cordia! Concordia!

D. B. CLARKE
Excuse me?

ADMINISTRATOR 3
That actually is an incredible idea for a name.

D. B. CLARKE
Agreed. But we're going to have to come up with a better origin story.

ADMINISTRATOR 2
(chanting) Fair is foul, and foul is fair. Hover through the fog and filthy air. Concordia! Concoooordiaaaa!!

D. B. CLARKE
I really don't know about you sometimes.

ADMINISTRATOR 3
But there is method to the madness. And now we have a way forward!

They exit, so energized as to almost appear sober.

SCENE 27

The PLAYERS converge for the ritual. It is a call and response between PLAYER 6 and the company, and this is a sacred ritual of remembering. PLAYER 6 returns to the CHORUS, PLAYER 7 and 8 are together with two calabashes, one filled with water. 7 pours, 8 holds the bowl receiving the water. After every name, they pour out some water into the other and with the chorus say "Ase."

PLAYER 7, 8, 6
We remember you. / We honour you. / We see you. / We thank you.

PLAYER 6, CHORUS
(everytime)
Ase

PLAYER 5
I was invited to your house for dinner.
So here I am.
I'm waiting on the doorstep, flowers in hand.

PLAYER 7
Terrence Ballantyne. Ase.

PLAYER 1
I see the lights on inside.
I know you're at home.
I ring the bell. It chimes.

PLAYER 8
Allan Brown. Ase.

PLAYER 2
The lights inside go out. I ring again. Silence now. The curtains close.

PLAYER 7
Oliver Chow. Ase.

PLAYER 4
I ring again. The doorbell is now a buzzer.
It stings me.
Still I knock politely. No answer.

PLAYER 8
Kennedy "Omowale" Frederick. Ase.

PLAYER 3
Did I get the date wrong?
Are my flowers not impressive enough?
How can I leave now when I've come all this way?

PLAYER 7
Rodney John. Ase.

PLAYER 1
I knock again. The streetlights extinguish.
I knock louder. The front gate locks behind me.
I pound on the door.

PLAYER 8
Douglas Mossop. Ase.

PLAYER 5
The door opens. The gate opens.
Soldiers pour in, pour out, surround me.

PLAYER 7
Mervyn Phillips. Ase.

PLAYER 3
My host is a firing squad.

ENSEMBLE
I cannot advance.
I may not retreat.

PLAYER 2, 1
Heart pounding, breath bounding / Blood ringing in my ears
I push down my fear.

PLAYER 8
Roosevelt Douglas. Ase

PLAYER 5, 3
I must be imagining things / I didn't show up empty-handed
Why am I no longer wanted here?

PLAYER 7
Lyne Bynoe. Ase.

PLAYER 1, 4
I'm given a cloth. Not a dinner napkin, but a blindfold. / The count-
down begins.
I realize.

PLAYER 8
Maurice Barrow. Ase.

PLAYER 2, 3
I'm not invited to dinner. / I am the feast.
Their favourite recipe.

PLAYER 7
Wendell K. Goodin. Ase.

PLAYER 4
I see the trembling fear and weakness desperate to cloak itself in violence
Smell the stench of shame and self-hatred
Hear the growls of insatiable hunger

PLAYER 8
Anne Cools. Ase.

PLAYER 1
Surrounded but isolated
Far from my home and my own
Hoodwinked and bamboozled
Heart sinking like stone

PLAYER 7
Brenda Dash. Ase.

PLAYER 5
Why didn't I walk away sooner
What should I have said or done to avoid this
To turn down the role of victim/surrogate/sacrifice
In this twisted fantasy

PLAYER 8
Yvonne Greer. Ase.

PLAYER 3
To whom can I appeal
If you look at me and only see
An animal, an Object
Your fuel

PLAYER 7
Andrew "Bukka" Rennie. Ase.

PLAYER 2
What can I do
When you refuse
To look at me
And see that I am also you

PLAYER 8
Kelvin Robinson. Ase.

PLAYER 1
To whom can I cry
When those who surround me
Refuse to hear me?

PLAYER 7
Coralee Hutchison. Ase.

PLAYER 3
Whatever happens next
I know this much is true

ENSEMBLE
I cannot keep silent

PLAYER 8
LeRoy Butcher. Ase.

PLAYER 4
Let me choose my own words
Même en franglais, osti
C'est à moi la parole maintenant
Pis tu sais que tu me comprends quand même très fucking bien

PLAYER 7
Philippe Fils-Aimé. Ase.

PLAYER 2
Because my voice resounds
The frequency of me
Can split heaven and earth down to its very soul

PLAYER 8
Bromley Armstrong. Ase.

PLAYER 4
Sound travels.
It doesn't fall.
It rebounds.

PLAYER 7
Viola Desmond. Ase.

PLAYER 5
My voice joins the chorus of the ancestors
In concert with the earth
And can never be destroyed

PLAYER 8
Marie-Josèphe Angélique. Ase.

PLAYER 3
Unless I stifle it.
So I won't keep quiet
I will be heard, because I am not alone

ALL
Olivier Le Jeune. Ase.

PLAYER 7, 8
Though many won't listen /
Others will hear /
Ma'at

> *In actually saying the name Ma'at (means justice, balance), it
> should become the call from the* CHORUS, *whose response is a
> song taken up by the* ENSEMBLE. *The "M" of Ma'at begins as
> a hum which gets taken up by the entire company to establish
> a drone, 528hz, which will underscore the spoken word and
> serves as the basis for the next section of the piece. The following
> five lines should become a spoken word piece that establishes a
> rhythm. It should incorporate breath as rests. It gets taken up by*

the entire company and progressively morphs into a collective
musical act of creation/invocation/chant/canon/call & response,
with elements of step dance and body percussion.

I am here/
I hear/
Here I am/
I am I/
I am

ENSEMBLE
Ase O!

AFTERWORD

BY RODNEY JOHN

The crisis at Sir George took place just over fifty-three years ago. Since then, I have had different opportunities to reflect and comment on the events. These have ranged from programs on CBC, to a film by the NFB, as well as discussions at various university campuses.

I remember feeling predominantly angry at what I had experienced and identified the experience as the arbitrary manner in which a white person could decide the trajectory of one's passage through life, essentially based on the colour of one's skin (or on the amount of blood that could reliably be measured).

At the fifty-year commemoration I attended a number of events, including the opening of the play *Blackout*. I left the play feeling a profound sense of sadness. The whole drama reflected the tragic absurdity of what it means to have human life codified through the lens of skin colour. The careers of the students that were derailed, the families disrupted, and the larger consequences unleashed on the Black community, the misuse of the justice system to punish us for having the temerity to seek social justice, to be treated fairly.

The latest event that demanded my reflection on the crisis was the launch of the final report of the president's task force on Anti-Black Racism; an apology for the university's response to the 1969 protests. This took place on October 28, 2022.

I was invited to the presentation as a representative of one of the six students who had signed the original complaint back in 1969. I felt a great deal of dissonance during the ceremony. I feel that it was appropriate for the university to acknowledge its responsibility, but I was in no position to respond on behalf of the literally hundreds of people whose lives had been negatively impacted.

At the ceremony it was noted that I had completed my degree at SGWU/ Concordia, and so I did. In point of fact, I eventually completed a PhD, a couple of MAS, a BA, and an LLM. However, the reality is that I have spent most of my post-1969 life dealing predominantly with the consequences of that event. I was headed towards medical school and that was derailed specifically because of Anderson being ably assisted by the institution which at that time had little interest in the principles of anti-racism.

I have often been asked whether or not things have changed. I am not quite sure what level of bigotry, discrimination, racism, and oppression of human rights should ever be acceptable.

When I left Saint Vincent in 1965, I came to Canada a Vincentian. Upon arriving in Canada, I discovered that I was, depending on the circumstances, a Negro or a Coloured person or a Ni—er, but never a full citizen. Later on, I became a Black person, or an African Canadian, but never, as white people are known, just a Canadian. To the extent that being white was the standard, and still is, people of colour are always required to prove themselves worthy of being. It is a situation that is both depressing and demoralizing and one that is not about to change anytime soon. It is evident that the privileges associated with being white will not be relinquished readily and that is clearly understood. People who wield power do not easily give it up.

I have no facile solutions to the issues, I have no expectation that things will change during my lifetime (I am not being cynical). The problem is that when institutions are held responsible for racism, it allows individuals to avoid responsibility for their behaviour.

The reality, as I see it, is that it is up to the marginalized sectors of the society to say enough, no more.

Rodney John is one of the original students who brought charges against Professor Perry Anderson back in 1968. He is retired from working as a psychologist and a mediator, and currently he lives in Toronto.

AFTERWORD

BY NANTALI INDONGO

When I sat in the audience of one of the performances of *Blackout*, I witnessed the learning.

From the performers, I saw the years of training to be thespians; their talents and skills seamlessly combining to embody characters who were real people, in a story that was once real, too.

I heard in the dialogue, the mind of the writers, poets, and dramaturgs fast at work interpreting facts and real events into emotive language and clever scene work.

I witnessed the learning from the audience, captivated like me, by this powerful and necessary work. Unlike me, many in the audience were hearing the story for the first time.

Unlike me, they were gasping at the blatant injustices for the first time. Unlike me, they were learning a part of Canadian-Québec-Montréal-Black-Caribbean student history.

I am so grateful for *Blackout*. It cements itself in the archives of the documentation of what was known as the "Sir George Affair."

Newspapers reported the facts as told by those who were there. Films recounted the experience. Some books have published the meaning of the event and of those leading up to and after it.

This work of theatre art re-enacts the moment with creative license; using the imaginative space of play to create more access to empathy and as a result, to more learning.

If that is not the goal and primary purpose of all art, I'm not sure what else it could be.

Nantali Indongo is the host of The Bridge, *an arts and cultural program on CBC Radio One. Building her craft as an artist with Montreal rap group Nomadic Massive for seventeen years, she remains a solo emcee and vocalist known as Tali Taliwah. Nantali is the daughter of Viola Aduke Daniel and Omowale Indongo, formerly Kennedy Frederick.*

TIMELINE OF EVENT

FEBRUARY 1968

A senior lecturer in Professor Perry Anderson's class informs the professor that many of his Black students believe him to be prejudiced against them. Professor Anderson convenes a meeting with two of the students to discuss the matter.

FEBRUARY–APRIL 1968

The Black students notice no improvement in Professor Anderson's behaviour towards them.

APRIL 29, 1968

Many students visit Magnus Flynn, Dean of Students, to discuss discrimination in Professor Anderson's biology class, some of the students present at the meeting were not directly concerned.

MAY 1, 1968

A second meeting is held with Magnus Flynn, this time only with students directly concerned.

MAY 1, 1968

The students visit Dean of Science, Samuel Madras, who takes notes of the student's concerns in a document he calls the "Case of Negro Students."

MAY 1, 1968

A meeting is held between Samuel Madras and Dr. Macleod, the Head of Biology, the department in which Professor Anderson works.

MAY 5, 1968

Meeting between students, Perry Anderson, Magnus Flynn, Samuel Madras, Dr. Macleod, and Joan Richardson, the Financial Aid Officer and Advisor to Overseas Students. No official minutes were taken. Only Richardson kept longhand notes. Richardson claims to send their notes via internal mail to Vice-Principal Academic D. B. Clarke, though he claims to never receive them. Madras claims to have lost his "Case of Negro Students" document, but later finds it in his office drawer many months later.

JUNE 14, 1968
Report by Dean Madras sent to faculty and staff of the May 5th meeting in which he rejects claims of racism and dismisses the complainants' case. The note is never sent to the students, who only learn that their case was closed when they learn of Anderson's promotion in the fall.

OCTOBER 11–14, 1968
The Congress of Black Writers is held at McGill University.

DECEMBER 5, 1968
Students intercept Principal Robert Rae and demand he terminate Perry Anderson, who in turn tells them to speak to Dr. Macleod. Not wishing to be dismissed, the students ask Principal Rae to be with them for said meeting. Principal Rae later notes that he felt threatened during this interaction, and that the students forcibly "escorted" him to the meeting with Dr. Macleod.

DECEMBER 8, 1968
Science faculty ask for police protection when they see Kennedy Frederick, one of the complainants, on school grounds.

DECEMBER 12, 1968
A meeting between complainants and the university is held to discuss the composition and process of a hearing committee to review the students' charges against Anderson. Two Black professors, Professors Bayne and Davis, are named to the committee. Principal Rae resigns. D. B. Clarke is named Interim Principal.

DECEMBER 16, 1968

D. B. Clarke gives Dean Madras until January 3, 1969, to work with the students and ensure the precise nature of their allegations is written down. If this deadline wasn't met, students would produce charges of their own by January 11th.

JANUARY 6, 1968

Vice-Principal Academic John O'Brien writes a letter to Professor Anderson warning of the "potential difficulties that may arise" should he resume teaching, and of the "risk of violence."

JANUARY 10, 1968

Students sign their formal charges: "We, the undersigned students, accuse Assistant Professor Anderson of racism."

JANUARY 22, 1969

Students confront John O'Brien in his office about his warnings of "risk of violence." He refutes the claim at first, but when students produced the letter, he acknowledges that he did write the words. The students request that he retract his statement in writing and mention that he is not doing so under duress.

JANUARY 22, 1969

Professors Bayne and Davis resign from the hearing committee, citing the ineffectiveness of the committee as a means of providing a solution to the conflict between the students and the university. The university chooses their replacements without consulting the complainants.

JANUARY 23, 1969

Unlawful confinement charges are brought against the students after the confrontation in O'Brien's office.

JANUARY 23, 1969

The complainants object to the hearing committee on the grounds that its composition has been unilaterally decided by the university.

JANUARY 29, 1969

All of the complainants as well as about two hundred other students walk out of the hearings in protest and occupy the Computer Centre on the ninth floor of the Hall Building.

FEBRUARY 6, 1969

The occupation expands to the seventh floor faculty lounge of the Hall Building.

FEBRUARY 10, 1969

The complainants and the university reach an agreement in principle to end the occupation. Protesters begin to leave the premises.

FEBRUARY 11, 1969

After many protesters have left, the university reneges on the agreement. The remaining protesters barricade themselves on the ninth floor, and the university sends in the riot police. Nintey-seven students are arrested. Several of the arrested students faced criminal charges, some were jailed, or even deported.

ABOUT THE AUTHORS

Tamara Brown is an award-winning multidisciplinary performing artist and creator based in Montreal who acts, sings, directs, and writes poetry for both the stage and screen. An occasional educator and perpetual student with a love for storytelling, natural sciences and the environment, alchemy, geekery, harmony, and social justice, Tamara is one of the founding members of Metachroma Theatre, created to address the under-representation of IBPOC artists in Quebec and Canadian theatre since 2010. Her work as a director has been seen on stages in Montreal, Toronto, Sherbrooke, Winnipeg, New York, and Stratford.

Kym Dominique-Ferguson is a poet by birth, a theatre performer and filmmaker by training, and a producer by nurture. For over a decade he has serenaded Montreal and international audiences with his blend of spoken-word poetry and theatre. He successfully produced and performed his first one-man show to a sold-out audience back in August of 2015: *The Born Jamhaitianadian*. Ferguson has also been a radio host on *Soul Perspectives*, CKUT 90.3FM, since 2012, a show that talks about the issues affecting the Black community in Montreal, across Canada, and internationally. He is honoured to be working on the development for his first play, *The #DearBlackMan Project*, officially commissioned by Black Theatre Workshop.

Lydie Dubuisson is a playwright, director, and curator from Tiohtià:ke/Montreal. She studied theatre and graduated with distinction from Concordia University. Her work examines intersectionality, dystopian reality, collective memory, and multilingual creative processes. Dubuisson wrote *Quiet/Silence* (2018 Discovery Series, Black Theatre Workshop and Maison de la culture NDG), *Sanctuary/Sanctuaire* (Black Theatre Workshop and Théâtre Aux Écuries), and *Sharing Our Stories, Telling Our Lives* (Teesri Duniya Theatre). She is currently writing a play about the Shelburne riots.

Mathieu Murphy-Perron is an award-winning producer, playwright, and director. He is the co-founding artistic director of Tableau D'Hôte Theatre. He served as co-idéateur of all the company's projects, alongside co-founder and former artistic director Mike Payette, from 2005–2016, before moving forward with his singular vision for the company after Payette's departure. Playwrighting credits include *Journey to Exodus*, *Return to Sender*, *PrAgression*, *Blackout*, and *En Pointe*, an episodic bilingual series of 20+ short street plays staged since the pandemic. His directorial aesthetic is heavily focused on heightened movement, physical humour, ensemble work, and imagery of collectiveness, resistance, and defiance.